LANA DEL REY

HER LIFE IN 94 SONGS

SQUINT

LANA DEL REY

HER LIFE IN 94 SONGS

THE EARLY CLASSICS

WITH A FOREWORD BY LISA MARIE BASILE

F.A. MANNAN

 **EYEWEAR** PUBLISHING

First published in 2016
Revised edition 2020
by The Black Spring Press Group
Suite 333, 19-21 Crawford Street
Marylebone, London W1H 1PJ
United Kingdom

Typeset with graphic design by Edwin Smet
Author photograph by Serena Bolton Photography

ISBN 978-1-913606-19-0

WWW.EYEWEARPUBLISHING.COM

SQUINT

BRIEF BOOKS FOR A BUSY WORLD
Look More Closely

F.A. Mannan holds a Bachelor of Arts in Computer Science from Cambridge and a Master of Music in Songwriting from Bath Spa. His thesis was on academic notions of authenticity in 'Born To Die' by Lana Del Rey. From London, he has worked both as a software engineer and a sound engineer.

CONTENTS

FOREWORD

As a poet, I've always been attracted to Lana Del
Rey's sonic abundance; beyond the orchestral
wall of sound, there's a woman who gives us truth,
vulnerability, detail, and nuance. For me, that's how
we make something immortal, memorable, and
meaningful. Lana Del Rey builds a luscious world,
and every time I listen in, as though with ears
pressed to a shell, I find myself in it, too – sad and
sexual and slipping between reality and another
time.

Lana's interest in the poetic and the literary –
which I first recognized in her *Lolita* obsession –
is as understated as it is enticing. It's hard not
to adore someone who, unlike the rest of the
monolithic industry, wants to swim in Beat poetry
and Whitman's verse. Her literary references are
consistent album to album, but I'm compelled by
the way she comes back to poetry: what is a poem?
A poem is a glimpse. It's a look between the lines.
It's the granular. When Lana quotes T.S. Eliot's
'Burnt Norton', it's her preoccupation with time and
chance and otherworld that we see. I adore this way
in which she always gives her listeners a glimpse,
a strange silence, an unrequited understanding,

a small detail. It's hard not to think that she's championing the poetic cause, and it's hard not to think that she's creating her own kind of sonic poetry.

To me, this artistic and intangible otherworld she creates is what makes Lana such a force. I witnessed this firsthand in the dumpy, debauched black hole known as Atlantic City, New Jersey, where Lana played at The Borgata, an ominously fake and ludicrous club with endless martinis that sits on the beach of my hometown. It is a place of Casino dreams and drug abuse and never knowing whether the sun is rising or falling. What better place to see Lana Del Rey?

In the intimate standing room, I watched as Lana swayed in and out of view of the close-up cameras, quiet and shy. She seemed almost uncomfortable, but then I had to remember what it takes to actually look people in the eye while admitting sins and flaws.

The whole way home, I tried to stitch together her persona, her lyrics, her stage-presence. I felt I needed to understand her, but then this elusive, imperfect wavelength is Lana's strength. Maybe there's not much to understand; maybe it's all about how she makes us feel.

Driving down that long stretch of highway aptly couched in the Pine Barrens, I thought that, if I could, I'd write a whole book on Lana, including all of the glamour and self-objectification and obsessive love that make up such a splendid and flawed woman. And that's what F.A. Mannan does here, opening the world of Lana's songwriting to us. Lana's work – and this guide – is something I will turn to again and again, seeing some new detail every time.

LISA MARIE BASILE

INTRODUCTION

Lana Del Rey is a singer: she brings songs to life. But her life is in the songs. These songs create a fertile fantasy America, populated with all manner of broken icons and aching souls. In this world, wherever you look – from the backwater fringes to the arterial freeways, from the mansions of Bel Air to New Jersey trailer parks – you find Lana herself. She has lived a life that is full and expansive, yet she has lived it quietly and contemplatively.

This is a travelogue of songs from way back in the buried mythic past, up to the online omnipresence of the current day. She goes by many names and values freedom and adaptability, but she revisits the same themes and people compulsively. Her songs are a tool she uses to reflect on her life, but they are also an artistic statement. If followed to the end, this journal leads the reader to a complete perspective on the songs of Lana Del Rey.

SONGS

I travel through the main works by Elizabeth Grant
and her alter egos, in chronological order. I omit
over a hundred unreleased songs from various
points in her career – mostly the later stages –
as they are usually subsumed by the released
material. With each song we will see her approach
a complete understanding of both her authorial and
her physical voice. Song audio, video and lyrics can
all be found online.

In the music industry, it is common for artists to
collaborate widely with co-writers and producers
(often the same person), generating as much
material as possible, with a view to culling it later.
Burt Bacharach recommends that your ratio of
written to released material be 3:1. That is, if you
want to release an album of ten songs, you write
forty and choose the ten that make the best album
(if you're Bruce Springsteen) or the ten best
individual singles (if you're Justin Bieber). Both
are valid approaches that optimise for different
things – Springsteen famously wanted *Darkness On
The Edge Of Town* to be proof that he was "great"
rather than make him rich or famous. Conversely,

a modern pop artist targeting casual fans and streaming users, who will probably never listen to the album all the way through, may treat an album as a collection of independent songs, aiming for each track to maximise its chart position. Once they have achieved fame they can then make more conceptually strong or complex statements.

Working with a diverse range of collaborators is faster and can also take the artist to places they would not have reached by themselves – but it risks diluting their original vision. In my opinion, Lana manages to avoid this skilfully. For example, Lana was carrying the title 'Brooklyn Baby' around at least as early as the *Born To Die* writing sessions, trialling it with different producers. However, it wasn't until the *Ultraviolence* sessions that an acceptable realisation of that title was created. This discipline and sense of artistic vision has enabled her to collaborate extensively, making the required concessions to modern pop music, but without losing her unique vision in the froth of hipness.

Given that Lana draws from the intersection of her own life experiences with a small, rich vein of popular culture, it is no surprise that many of the tracks overlap thematically – of course, even the released tracks re-tread the same lyrical, melodic and atmospheric territory – but these overlaps are an intentional part of the process of developing a thematically consistent body of work, so it would be unfair to accuse Lana of repetitiveness based on demos that were never meant to be heard (although I will make reference to the titles of unreleased tracks when they reveal pertinent information about her universe). The deep intertextuality of her work serves to generate a more cohesive world.

Young like me | Rock me stable

The earliest known relevant work is April 25th 2005's seven-track CD registered in the US Copyright Office to Elizabeth Woolridge Grant.

The production is transparent – these tracks could be home recordings. The incredibly strong themes that emerge in her later work are only here as inklings in what seems to be a fairly unaffected, if slightly unhinged, collection of songs. Readers can find the songs here scattered around the web (often on YouTube or SoundCloud).

At this point in time, Elizabeth has graduated boarding school and spent a year waitressing and living with her aunt and uncle in Long Island. Her uncle taught her to play guitar, and lo, her schoolgirl singing skills and poetic ambitions finally coincided. Lana's childhood ambition was to be a poet. As a poet and singer, therefore, her focus is on the words, rather than the guitar playing – in this way, she echoes Leonard Cohen and Lou Reed.

Later on, as more producers and co-writers get involved, the tracks will become astonishing in all possible ways, rather than being a vehicle for poetry, but Elizabeth will hold onto her authorial integrity: in the modern co-writing world, singers who co-write with a lot of people often retain primary control and, informally, the last word on the lyrics.

These are her first steps into songwriting. During this period she enrols at Fordham University, where she will major in philosophy, having turned down the State University of New York at Geneseo (a campus of SUNY) the previous year.

Blizzard

The song is quiet and reflective, built on major chords in the folk tradition. The topline (what songwriters call the vocal melody and lyric) has a rambling feel, although there is a clear verse/chorus structure. Elizabeth sings in her comfortable range, restrained and slightly delicate, sometimes even modulating into speech. You can hear her smile. The tone when she describes her Friday evening is interestingly formal and religious. Elizabeth expresses nostalgia for when she was in high school. The blizzard could be a literal weather condition in Lake Placid, the sleepy winter holiday village where Elizabeth was raised, as well as signifying being snowed under in one's personal life.

She immediately showcases her way of altering her vocal tone mid-note. Listeners will recognise that later on, when she has fully become Lana Del Rey, this technique is much more developed and powerful. Note the conversational register and mundane activities like shopping and eating out with friends – these are very relatable but not interesting, and will be cut out as Elizabeth develops her authorial voice.

The male subject could be an old friend or ex-boyfriend who was too depressive to sustain the relationship. She talks about her independence from him, in terms of both mood and actions. It raises an important point about her choice of partners: she has said in interviews that she chooses older men simply because they are more self-assured than men her own age, which she finds attractive (compare the Amy Winehouse song 'Stronger Than Me'), and here she is already showing that she doesn't really want to be dealing with the qualms and baggage of her partners. In interviews she maintains that she is happy and grateful every day, despite the sad, aching quality of the songs. They aren't mutually exclusive.

You, Mister

Elizabeth's voice in this track hits glittering high notes. The song is a cerebral analysis of her confession of her feelings for someone, and she talks about using techniques like visualisation to control her emotions. The guitar is solemnly, somewhat clumsily, fingerpicked – the chords hint at a pleasant, slightly jazzy harmony that isn't fully realised – it gets dragged back to static plucking. The overall impression is dreamy and indistinct.

This song reveals her overthinking, almost neurotic tendencies. The reader will see that these are toned down as time passes – and this is not altogether unsurprising: although anyone from any time could be an overthinker, confessing these thoughts in songs still seems slightly too modern to survive the transformation to Lana Del Rey. "Confessional" singer-songwriters, male and female, have periodically seen massive commercial success, but something about that style does not mesh with the wandering-jazz-singer tropes that will later dominate Lana's chosen aesthetic. She will choose to lyrically focus on more physical things and signifiers and downplay the abstract and emotional lyrics (although of course the emotions remain,

but all compressed into her voice and the music –
that will take her further from poetry). This is not
to say that her aesthetic will become exclusively
anachronistic – but that it is a delicate balance.

Junky Pride

In this song Elizabeth baldly states that this
relationship is breaking down – and she's
outgrowing her boyfriend. Her own visions for her
future are much larger in scope than his addiction-
dominated worldview. The chords and melody have
their moments, but not too many at the same time
– however, the construction of the hook is musically
quite brilliant, and there are very pleasing melodic
sub-hooks throughout.

Interestingly, the hook lyric scans lopsidedly over
the music, which could be the result of writing the
lyrics first as standalone poetry and then adapting
them to a section of music without wanting to
edit them to fit. The effect is less refined than
the meticulously layered music of her later work
– but it also imparts an undeniable charm and
sense of sincerity. This song has no discernible
affectation or artifice at all (apart from the intrinsic
contrivance of being a song). Her later songs, while

just as factual in their subject matter, will be so polished and deal in such archetypal themes that people who haven't experienced similar things will have a hard time believing they are real (note that the same is true of all love songs, which mostly seem idiotic or at least baffling until one has been in love).

Move / Find My Own Way

From the weather-related imagery, it seems we are in Lake Placid again. She may be talking about doing cocaine or crying habitually when she talks about how her behaviour mirrors the weather. Her characteristic acoustic guitar chords are not fingerpicked this time – they are strummed, slightly haltingly.

She talks to a lover about drugs delivered in a slanged-up way that foreshadows what's to come regarding her lyrical registers. She asserts her independence and devil-may-care attitude by discussing her confidence about making her journey home by herself. These two facets of her personality will remain prominent themes in her work. She immediately juxtaposes this self-assurance with the physical and emotional symptoms of a nervous panic attack: she hasn't yet resigned herself to being a self-contained lost soul. The nostalgic connection to her hometown is palpable in this song.

Elizabeth went to Catholic school as a child, and it certainly left its mark – not unlike her hero Bruce Springsteen (she has even described herself as "Bruce Springsteen in Miami"), who was profoundly affected by his Catholic school experience. She was the *cantor* in her school choir – the lead singer, in a sense: she would sing solo passages (she would also sing at home with her mother).

Elizabeth makes a fairly big appeal to Jesus: she wants him to come back to humanity. The presentation of Jesus as a very mortal man is common, but coming from Elizabeth it seems like it could be a Whitmanesque pantheistic remark. While classical singing is certainly a different beast to pop, the melismatic runs are examples of her vocal agility, which will be deployed fully before too long.

There's Nothing to be Sorry About

In pleasant, legato tones, Elizabeth talks about
how the young man she has been in love with
has changed for the worse. A traumatic incident
befell him half a year ago and now he is unhinged.
She wants to help but he's shutting her out. She
appeals to God to watch over him, and then takes it
a step or two further, declaring that she would stop
at nothing to assist him, and finally pledges herself
to help anyone in need. The theme of throwing
herself into the lives of other people will continue
to grow in her life and work.

The theme of driving, essential to the both
archetypal America and Elizabeth's own life,
is here, but on the sidelines. She may not have
done any long road trips yet. Elizabeth seems
perturbed by her discovery that most people have a
companion – she hasn't yet fully accepted the loner
mentality.

More Mountains

The vocals are pretty and reaching higher and
further from Elizabeth's comfortable range. Her

discussion of the open-ended, irreducible nature of life suffers from a clumsy identity rhyme but retains a thrillingly nihilistic concept. On the whole, this is a wistful, airy, impressionistic song. She sensibly admonishes her lover for being too depressive. She goes on to contemplate the possibility of an immortal soul via a mishmash of philosophy, abstract images and religious references. Heavenly bodies will recur in her work.

In Wendy

Contrary to her later work, Elizabeth assures herself that she is mentally normal. She reveals the people-pleasing part of her personality that will be pathological by the time we get to *Born To Die*'s 'Carmen'. The song appears to be about both a brief respite from depression and simultaneously catching up with an old flame. She admits some kind of vulnerability, no longer believing herself to be rock-solid – combined with the affirmation of her sanity, this is a realistic take on an aspect of the human experience. She emphasises her humanity.

Coming from anyone else, the line about being a different person would simply be a melodramatic or ship-of-Theseus-inspired way of expressing that cumulative changes had built up and transformed them. Since it's Elizabeth, on the cusp of turning into May Jailer, it suggests a goodbye to her old personality, persona or lifestyle.

From the end

Out With a Bang

This song is a suicide note.

Sarasota is in Florida – Elizabeth finds the weather there to be judgmental. She ascribes positive traits to a tornado at home in Oklahoma: an interesting way of talking about being in her natural environment – one that quietly accepts that some entities are naturally destructive, as an intrinsic part of their character.

Elizabeth uses the definite article when talking about strangers, which hints at a way of thinking about people as archetypes and icons rather than individual agents. Her boyfriends all play a rôle, as does she. However this is a red herring. In the fourth verse, despite – or because of – her lover finding her, she ends up dead: they both drown. She talks about her anxiety.

The final chorus changes from being only about her to being about the couple – this upgrades the note to a suicide pact. The last line about returning home suggests the afterlife or perhaps the ground – Catholic or pantheistic, either one works!

Peace / All You Need

This song starts with a call to realise your own unique nature and to live fully – like Lord Henry's advice to Dorian Gray. But it seems that Elizabeth's real situation remains peaceful and almost boring, to the point of melancholy. The delivery of Elizabeth's thoughts about making one's dreams into reality is shockingly sad. The hook lurches down into a well-placed minor chord on the guitar.

She seems to be talking to a close friend (she hears the friend's voice in her sleep). She knows ultimately that she wants to be out there on the road, experiencing positive things, but right now she isn't. She seems to be consoling a travelling friend who is stopping over at home for a break. The details of the persons involved and points of view aren't totally clear, but the theme is.

The occasionally rushing scansion is a little jarring given the beauty of the rest of the song but could signify her inner unrest. Overall, she tinges the idea of following one's dreams with a pre-emptive homesickness, nostalgia and regret.

Bad Disease

Elizabeth confesses that crime makes her greedy and that seeing her boyfriend fight makes her want to party. This lust for violence and danger seems to be the disease, but each verse reveals a little more. The second verse plummets: her boyfriend dies. Now she wants to stay at home and be by herself. She is deeply depressed and very restless. She knows drinking isn't the answer – the disease now seems to be alcoholism. She has talked about alcoholism as being the main malady of her youth, for which her parents sent her to Kent School. It was successful and she has been cured. In interviews she has said that some of her songs that seem to be about men are simply about alcohol, but I suspect the truth is more mixed. Songwriting is an act of synthesis, and since 100% factual accuracy can never be established, credibility is the only usable proxy for authenticity.

In this song, Elizabeth's voice is mainly clear but sometimes has a deep, vocal edge and other times has the nasal quack that she will use in her rap-like sections on the *Born To Die* album. The song is structurally invigorated by the second chorus being much higher than the first, but interestingly

Elizabeth will later stick to her lower tones much more, for a less generic sound. By the end of this song, we can hear that no-one will help her. Distressingly, she seems to call out to the listener in a final plea.

For You / For Charlie

Here, Elizabeth writes off having feelings and emotions altogether, but still she talks about trying to keep her relationship together. Like the others, this song betrays a slight country influence, both in melody and vocal accent and even with the use of the words for workingmen, like an old, "real" country song about being a normal working person. Over the course of the song, she changes the list of innocuous workingmen to a list of murderers and arsonists— a hint of the escalating carnage she dreams about. We hear her capacity to move on and to rise above envy – a crucial skill given that in future scenarios, other women will often be involved.

Some lines are delivered in a very hooky, poppy way, a revelation of Elizabeth's very canny melodic sensibility. The call for pride, and to come out, has gay undertones and indicates that there is additional subtext. Given that an alternate title for the song given online is 'For Charlie', which could be a reference to her younger brother Charlie (not to be confused with her sister Chuck), that line may be aimed at him.

Wait

This song implores someone male – again possibly Charlie – not to grow up too fast. She doesn't want him to be out on the streets like she is. Although she loves living an alternative, peripheral lifestyle, in this song and even as late as 'Carmen' on *Born To Die*, she world-wearily advises others not to imitate her.

The vocals are tonally varied, with an emphasised accent and slightly quacky tone present in this song. Although she talks about kissing the subject, maybe it's non-romantic as she is not known to like men younger than herself (older men don't need to worry about not growing up too fast). Elizabeth's reservoir of self-assurance and independence extends to him as well as she elucidates her faith that he is capable of anything, again suggesting that he is family or at least very close.

How Do You Know Me So Well? /
I'm Indebted to You

The initial acoustic guitar tone, strange major chords and playing together sound similar to the Cuban classical guitarist Leo Brouwer. It could even be a nylon strung guitar instead of the steely, loud American style. Her vocals are getting deeper here, and are ornamented, especially on the post-hook payoff lyric. The song is a story about a couple who initially seem similar because they both have significant hidden facets to their personalities. It seems like when the woman figures out the man, he is affronted and breaks up with her.

Elizabeth goes into the first person for the hook line which seeks to express that it was a relationship that had a positive impact on her overall. She learned something – and seems to be passing on a lesson to us: it's risky to hurt this man's pride.

Try Tonight

Elizabeth's voice here takes on the quack it will have on the *Born To Die* album. She talks about her boyfriend's obsession with clichés and his self-centred sense of tragedy. Mentioning clichés directly in the lyrics here strikes me as too meta, and a hallmark of her pre-stylisation phase. Elizabeth herself will take on both of these traits (embracing tropes and sense of tragedy) as her persona develops.

She is with a man who chronically refuses to cheer up, and wants to love him and make him happy. An alternative interpretation is that she wants to dominate him: she wants to make him smile and ends up boasting that she'll force him to get high, against his will. This is a classic sexual thought expressed via the tropes of emotions and drugs.

This song is conceptually similar to 'Black Beauty' from *Ultraviolence:* listening to the two back-to-back is instructive and brings the differences between an Elizabeth Grant song and a Lana Del Rey song into sharp relief.

Dear Elliot / Westbound

In this less affected performance, Elizabeth is again upfront over a simple harmony. Crucially, she accepts that writing about problems in song doesn't solve them (at least not directly). The song is rambling and folky. She laments the breakup, as she still loves her ex. She seems to be in classic post-breakup denial and oscillates in her assessment of him. There is little specific detail and in fact she is rather flippant here, at one point even calling him an annoyance. We find out that he's an archetypal bad boy – this will become her type over the years. As someone sensitive and thoughtful, she will experience obvious downsides with that sort of partner, but the positives of having a self-assured partner will soon outweigh the negatives for Elizabeth as she grows more confident.

Drive By / Sirens / For K Part 1

This song sounds like a traditional murder ballad, an effective retro reference. The way we hit a minor chord during a critical, held vocal note is very effective songwriting. The title character, K, was apparently sentenced to 30 years and then to death in a retrial, for murdering two people in a drive-by shooting.

This song is obviously pivotal for Elizabeth as it will go on to be the title track of *Sirens* (when she will be known as May Jailer). Indeed, she seems to have felt so close to K that she felt she was physically locked up with him. While she doesn't mention a relationship here, later it will become apparent that they were together.

In the song she discusses how he was kind and intelligent, but was motivated by money to break the law. The lesson of this experience – that nice, bright people can drop out of mainstream society – will echo in her life and work. She herself chooses an alternative lifestyle, and her choice to work in homeless outreach and alcohol and drug rehabilitation shows her empathy and affinity for those marginalised by mainstream society.

Aviation

Elizabeth's vocals are here adorned with hummingbird-like trills and turns on the ends of phrases. She candidly talks about how her philosophy degree hasn't really helped her decide what to do with her life. In interviews she has talked about how she chose philosophy because she wanted to ponder the big questions in the company of people with similar interests. Sadly that kind of atmosphere cannot exist unscrutinised outside a university environment.

The lyric tells her parents that she wishes to escape her loneliness by flying away from New York to Pensacola, Florida (additionally, the reference to military aircraft carries the essence of that classic, paradoxical rich kid rebellion: joining the army). She expresses the fundamental wish of the nomad – to be able to start her life again.

The avian tendencies of this song will become part of the bigger fabric of her first LP, *Sirens*. The fact that she deliberately chose an aeronautical angle (rather than an automotive one) shows that she could sacrifice the obvious choice in favour of one that would lead to a more cohesive album. This is a major part of having a consistent, clear artistic voice.

Sirens

Under the name May Jailer, this is the first LP, mostly derived from the previous two EPs with some new material. An acoustic, birdlike collection of songs, it reaches beyond the EPs to start forming a cohesive vision, but not the final one. The album was released online and pulled soon after.

May begins to use the word "daddy" and more frankly discusses her preference for older men, often philanderers, evoking a connection to Sylvia Plath. Plath's suicide, and the death of Assia Wevill (who Plath's husband Ted Hughes cheated with, and who killed herself and her child after Plath's death), definitely inform the sense of love and death in May's songs.

Drive By / Sirens / For K Part 1
As in *From The End*

Next to Me

May gives a birdlike vocal performance, replete with effective vibrato and runs. In this impressively crafted song, a deadpan Jailer extends an

ambiguous invitation to a married man. This is
the first time we see May as "the other woman",
although we don't get any details this time.

The man wearily talks about how he's lived life on
autopilot – sounds like he has sleepwalked into
a comfortable but unfulfilling life with a decent
house and a good wife (reminiscent of 'Once In
A Lifetime' by Talking Heads) – importantly, this
easy life is in total contrast to May's lifestyle.
We learn she has a taste for it by proxy, and later
she will deal with dreams of financial excess and
relationship bliss that she lives out through affluent
older boyfriends. This theme will be revisited in the
short film *Poolside* that May stars in as Lizzy Grant,
and will be present on *Born To Die*.

A Star For Nick

This is the first time artificial reverb features on a
track. All the tracks up to now sound like they could
have been home recordings but now we start to
hear how May's voice can interact with reverb. This
is the beginning of her transformation from May
Jailer into Lana Del Rey. With this atmospheric,
enveloping sense of space, the high notes ring like
bells and sound like distant, fragmentary siren
songs.

'A Star For Nick' sounds like a funeral song. Lyrically it starts with her confidently talking about her future as a star and how the addressee is holding her back. However, soon enough she is singing about her soul leaving her body. This suggests she sees attaining stardom as a spiritual process – an ascension, a rebirth... or at the very least a kind of death. This extreme, mystical and messianic way of looking at the world is only going to get stronger.

There is a slow *rallentando* in the ending guitar part, sounding almost Spanish or classical-guitar-influenced. This musical flourish exemplifies the increased variety and musicality of the production on *Sirens*.

My Momma

Here May comments to us that most of her boyfriends are unemployed and over forty and implies that this has messed up her relationship with her mother.

There is added reverb here as well – not at as extreme a level as used in 'A Star For Nick', but a more conventional amount. The sense of melody is more developed and far less rambling than the EP tracks. May sardonically implies her mother actually shares her taste in men, and the run at the end of the line about her mother falling for him is reminiscent of 'Jolene' melodically – a sly but strong reference. The line itself is disquieting.

The melody of this whole track is fantastic. The song ends on the parallel major chord, a surprising and affirmative move, reminiscent of the very end of 'Doolin' Dalton' by The Eagles, a song that will be referenced more directly in 'God Knows I Tried'.

Bad Disease

As in *From the end.*

Out With A Bang

As in *From the end.*

Dear Elliot

As in *From the end.*

Try Tonight

As in *From the end.*

Peace

As in *From the end.*

How Do You Know Me So Well?

As in *From the end.*

Pretty Baby

This is a great track, and the opening couplet –
both lyrically and in terms of vocal ability – says
it all. She talks about finally moving on from a
relationship in which she is not appreciated.
May introduces her soon-to-be-signature vocal
leaps into what would otherwise be a normal, if
impressively level-headed, break-up song. Her bad
boy lover is fast becoming an iconic character in
her universe.

The melancholy mood is now definitively making its
way into May's guitar work too: not only is the chord
progression more sophisticated – the entire song
is sadder and more refined structurally than the EP
tracks.

Aviation

As in *From the end.*

Move

As in *Young like me.*

Junky Pride

As in *Young like me.*

Birds Of A Feather

In this newly-written avian song, May expresses some mild disdain for L.A. people – she's a hardened New Jersey gal (who, as we learned in 'Aviation', has designs on Florida).

There is a slightly giddy, childish aspect here – she calls him nice and thinks his mother is hip. She likes Jimi Hendrix fans! She sounds infatuated, which may be why she excuses his chronic depression. While the selection of traits displayed here could apply to almost anyone – we all have ups and downs – the male character in this song is definitely less of a bad boy.

The title implies that this is how she sees herself: kind and strange. She hints at bisexual tendencies in her boyfriend, and by the 'Birds Of A Feather' argument, maybe hints at her having them too. Or maybe it means they just share an appreciation for male beauty. In her 'Summertime Sadness' video later, she appears as part of a lesbian couple.

Lana Del Ray (including *Kill Kill* EP)

Now referring to herself as "Lizzy Grant a.k.a. Lana Del Ray" [sic – the spelling will change from Ray to Rey in future], our heroine sent out a demo EP called *No Kung Fu* to numerous producers. It was a hit with David Kahne, who took up the job of producing the album. *No Kung Fu* contains a song called 'Jimmy Gnecco', about the titular musician, who Lizzy seems to have been in a serious relationship with. He is a strong presence throughout her work, and will recur as a visual trope in her videos and as a lyrical inspiration.

In 2007 Lizzy signed to 5 Points Records with a $10,000 advance, while a senior at Fordham. She used the money to rent a trailer in Manhattan Mobile Home Park in North Bergen, New Jersey. The deal, stipulating one album, was brokered by Van Wilson, who found Lizzy at her first performance in 2006 at the Williamsburg Live Songwriting Competition. She recorded the required album *Lana Del Ray a.k.a. Lizzy Grant* with her then-boyfriend, musician/producer Steve Mertens, but then scrapped the whole thing and re-recorded a new version with Kahne: almost every song on the album was written solely by Elizabeth Grant – the exceptions were 'Gramma (Blue Ribbon Sparkler Trailer Heaven', 'Pawn Shop Blues' and 'Smarty', which were co-written with Kahne.

However, the album was shelved. Lizzy went back to her work in homeless, drug and alcohol outreach. In 2008, the iTunes team reached out to 5 Points and offered to shine a virtual 'artist spotlight' on Lana – to capitalise and create some buzz, 5 Points went for it. The result was the release, on iTunes, of the *Kill Kill* EP – three songs from the stalled *Lana Del Ray a.k.a. Lizzy Grant* album. *Kill Kill*'s cover featured bright tropical colours around a blonde, sun-bathed Lizzy. Lizzy called the genre "Hawaiian glam metal" and cited the influence of Elvis, Poison and Van Halen.

Finally, the full album made it out in 2010. It was briefly for sale on iTunes before other events kicked in, catalysing Lana's final transformation. Here we leave behind May Jailer and her acoustic guitar. The production and aesthetic are about to go into overdrive. Her work with David Kahne was pretty extensive – he got the idea of it sounding "famous, like a sad party" – right on the money. This hedonistic streak, as yet unrealised, begins to manifest itself now.

In 2010 Lizzy had a lead role in *Poolside*, a short film made with her friends. The film can be viewed on YouTube and deals with themes like the emptiness of wealth, and the collision between wealthy people and the less wealthy. These themes will be revisited more explicitly by Lizzy, but not on this album.

The name Lana Del Ray (which will later be slightly revised and finalised to Lana Del Rey) has many connotations that give it a nostalgic, glamorous quality rooted in mythic Americana.

It conjures the spirit of Lana Turner, the film noir actress famed for her ingénue and femme fatale roles, and subject of a famous Frank O'Hara poem. Legend has it she was discovered – on account of her beauty – by William R. Wilkerson (publisher of *The Hollywood Reporter*). She was 16 at the time, playing hookey from typing class at Hollywood High School, and sipping Coca Cola at an ice cream parlour on Sunset Boulevard. She was signed to Zeppo Marx's talent agency and then to MGM. Her young age, and that Coke, have an eerie resemblance to *Lolita*. Turner suffered from depression for most of her life, had three stillbirths and two abortions, and became a devout Roman Catholic in her later years. She married eight times to seven husbands, saying she was more interested in romance than sex. She attempted suicide but ultimately died of throat cancer from smoking. A troubled soul indeed and a touchstone for our Lana.

The name also echoes Marina Del Rey, a harbour in L.A. county, California that was immortalised in the song of the same name by country juggernaut George Strait. The song deals with a love affair on the beach, which sounds like it could be one of Lana's songs. Her look begins to resemble that of Priscilla Presley, young wife of her hero Elvis, who was plaintive and sad before he became sexual and ultimately gaudy. "Del Rey" literally means "of the king" in Spanish.

Kill Kill

This track was originally called 'The Ocean' but this was regarded as too boring by David Kahne, causing Lizzy to angrily strike it out and write 'Kill Kill' instead.

She wonders whether he knows about the impending breakup. Her statement about her love being at death's door echoes a line from 'Move / Find My Own Way'. Is she quietly ascribing messianic qualities to her lover or just getting ready to crucify him? He seems to be dying of an addiction.

Lana sadly announces her intention to leave despite still being in love with him. As her voice leaps, we can hear that her vocal game has been upped once again. The equating of fading stars with death is interesting given the equating of stardom with death in 'A Star For Nick'. Either way, fame takes you away.

The 60s guitar stabs are very effective and will be heard again in 'Gods & Monsters' much later.

Queen of the Gas Station

This song has an upbeat, "driving" feel that matches the lyric meaning. In it, Lizzy lyrically displays self-awareness of her shapeshifting and her comfort with allowing others to fill in the blanks and project themselves onto her.

This track is much more developed in terms of thematic focus and instrumentation. The retro atmosphere built up by the music and the dense imagery is strong and immersive. The vocal is dry and upfront with a pronounced twang – Lizzy is on the prowl for men who might take her fancy. She is developing a direct and concrete language to give her abstract philosophising some corporeality (this is crucial in songwriting – being too abstract is the easiest way to write an unlikeable lyric).

The refrain is well constructed and well executed. It has the air of a 60s pop song full of too many major chords that somehow comes across wonky and twisted (think 'It's My Party' by Lesley Gore).

Oh Say Can You See

A direct reference to the American national anthem. The opening melody will be re-used in the song 'Yayo'.

A quietly sad descending acoustic guitar figure underpins a tasteful arrangement that will influence her songs to come. There are stirring and hymnal melodic fragments – the same rising melodic figure recurs with the blunt but effective Nirvana reference and sounds like religious veneration. The simpler lyrics indicate that Lizzy is learning that lyrics are not poetry – a good lyric can sound flat and almost idiotic on paper but when delivered in its musical context can be spine-tingling. The imagery about car headlights strongly evokes a sense of scene and motion.

The electric guitar part is a more overt period reference than will make it into the next album. There is a brief celestially escapist fragment which calls to mind Bowie's 'Life On Mars?'. The lyric about tiring as the night goes on suggests she's keeping an older man up all night.

Gramma (Blue Ribbon Sparkler Trailer Heaven)

The only track from Lizzy's MySpace (under the name Sparkle Jump Rope Queen) to see a physical release, the title of this song references the blue ribbons she would decorate her trailer with. This track is a dialogue between Lizzy and her grandmother.

The loving feelings for everyone that she expresses in the lyrics constitute a transcendent, pansexual Whitmanesque sentiment, and her fear of being hated for loving her own appearance touches on the hypocrisy women face regarding their appearance, self-image and choice of who to love.

The fluttering vibrato Lizzy uses on her oohs
and aahs in this song will become a signature
vocal technique in her repertoire, and the sinister
twinkling electric piano will find its way into more
of her tracks.

For K Part 2

Lizzy's accent is super strong in this song, and
she's waxing melancholic. Swaying lethargic
lounge guitar with open cymbals in the background
give way to xylophonic, *ostinato* interval hits. A
cello line descends...

She meets the handsome K in a bar where she's
performing. The chorus comes across unguarded.
The way she addresses him makes her sound
confident in a world-weary way – like she has seen
everything. It's revealing that she calls him by a pet
name that she will later use to refer to herself.

He's handsome and he can sing – and she's
enthralled by him. A generic term of excitement
but given her Whitman obsession, this could
be reference to the "body electric", which she
will later reference directly. Lizzy's vocals are

exposed, unaffected and intimate. The effect is very charming. She dares him to pick her up.

This fills in more of the backstory to K's death in 'For K Part 1'. He was a lover of hers, and a rock and roller, although 'Part 1' makes it seem like they had split by the time he went to prison.

Jump

This is an upbeat suicide track with 60s organs, handclaps, chunky drums and synth bass. Palm trees are the last thing she sees. This could place her in New Jersey, Florida or California. She talks about riding with her older, addict boyfriend in his cool car. The song talks about him crashing the car and presumably killing both of them (similar to what will happen in the 'Born To Die' video, although in that, the man isn't as visibly old and he actually survives while Lana dies).

Mermaid Motel

The track sounds insane at the start – the production is off-kilter and unsubtle: thick, honking "orchestral hit" sounds pound away. Strange sounds recur throughout the track and are not always effective, but this experimentation is a necessary part of the process of 'coining' a sound. The parallel vocal process also happens in this track, with Lizzy trying various different ways of using her voice, some technological and some organic.

Lizzy is feeling very American as she sings about Coney Island and the national anthem. Later she compares herself to Miss America. The Neptune Avenue she sings about here is in Coney Island, an infamous, run down New York seaside resort neighbourhood (it's so New York that it even gets a mention in the rarefied atmosphere of *The Great Gatsby*). They're heading back to a motel – so they've obviously been on the road.

The whispering is one of this track's instances of a willingness to experiment with extreme vocal textures. Sections are sung via a vocoder (a machine or nowadays piece of software that imperfectly simulates vocal harmonies, resulting in a grating but very distinctive robotic sound). The textures ease up in the chorus, with summer scents and sun: sweet but also somehow foreboding. The fragile harmonies are beautiful. The second time she sings about Coney Island, the vocals are intimate – they sound like they are being softly, emotionally spoken in the ear during an embrace. There's a sharp inhalation of breath later.

This song is self-aware to the point of acknowledging that Lizzy needs a purple wig for her music video. It seems to work for her given that this has been par for the course from the start in her work, but it's worth noting that most artists will play it safe and not break the fourth wall, presumably to make the songs more relatable and avoid cringe-worthy bragging. For example, Justin Bieber understatedly calls being a pop star his mere profession in 2015's snarky Bieber/Blanco/Sheeran co-write 'Sorry'.

One of Lana's tattoos is the word "Amy" after Amy Winehouse, who called herself Amy Jade Mermaid on social media. The idea of a mermaid also relates vaguely to the idea of a siren, as in *Sirens*, *Ultraviolence* and Lizzy herself.

Raise Me Up (Mississippi South)

The vocal production is ambitious on this track. The initial intro singing is processed through a delay special effect. The haunting, distant backing vocals are treated with ringing cathedral reverb. A rollicking rocky beat kicks in which Lana sings chattily and with vocal fry. The effect is brilliant, like a more aerated Nirvana. She sounds calmly sad and self-contained. The chorus does exactly what it's meant to, providing an aural lift. She whispers or otherwise lightens the note on specific words for pleasing moments of prosody.

A few beeps and distorted guitars do come in after a bit to liven up the sonic landscape, and when Lizzy starts to belt, we hear a rarely heard rock 'n' roll, Stevie-Nicks-like facet of her voice. In some lines, there are delicate, well-formed ad-libs in a Nirvana-like section of the song. The other slight hiccups and mini-yodels in her voice work well.

The lyrics contain imagery of spiritual items in the south. She is addressing a man – probably older, as in the last verse he has a CB walkie-talkie like in a 70s cop car. She wants to play with his radio and gun – both an innuendo and a slight self-infantilisation. Having said that, she sounds like she is in control. She jokingly blames him for making her fall for him.

Pawn Shop Blues

The plaintive plucked acoustic guitar forms a lush bed for the confident, well-developed and agile vocal performance. The song deals with Lizzy giving away the physical remnants of a failed relationship, ready to progress onto something new. She is nearly, but not quite, brought to tears. She doesn't care about living on next to no food, but her real cost of living is all about travel expenses. She has to be able to move.

The wordless chorus is a sad overgrown coo – a high, lonesome sound. Lizzy gets a bit mystical here, talking about the mind of God and a collective consciousness. In the rest of the lyrics she laments that her approach to relationships – that they are emphatically finite – is an unchangeable, unavoidable part of her personality and her life.

Brite Lites

The lyrics comprise cool, minimal lines, repeated. She has been in a relationship with someone famous. She talks about removing her wedding ring – maybe like the earrings in 'Pawn Shop Blues', she's both moving on and in need of some cash for gas. She is blunt about the simple devastation of the end of a giving love.

She demands the spotlight, repeating her refrain while still sounding noncommittal or conflicted – her vocal tone communicates some kind of apathy or sadness, suggesting that she is beginning to realise fame may not be enough (later, in 'Born To Die', love itself will not be enough).

The silver screen specifically refers to the silver lenticular screen, a projection screen popular in the early days of cinema. It predates Technicolor, for example. Although it is generically used to refer to all projection screens, "Stars of the silver screen" has a retro feel and brings to mind images of Audrey Hepburn and Marilyn Monroe, James Dean and Marlon Brando rather than Robert Pattinson or Jennifer Lawrence. The juxtaposition of the images of movie stardom with backyard games says something more. She is relating dreams of fame and Hollywood stardom with child's play – suggesting they are aspects of the same naivety.

Continuing with the movie star theme, Lana begs us to look at her before she fades away. These themes – the transience of youth and beauty, or the

ticking clock counting down 15 minutes of fame
– are recapitulated in 'Young and Beautiful'. She
talks about the same friends that she will reference
in 'This Is What Makes Us Girls' on *Born To Die*.

Lyrically, she moves through different phases
of the breakup. She accepts that the affair was
meaningless in the grand scheme of things, and
that she was equally meaningless to him. She talks
about a fictional school or university, but its name
is a corruption of Dean Arbour, a car dealership. So
it could mean a return to her nomadic lifestyle.

There is an old video re-upload of this song
available on YouTube, with grainy home-movie style
footage, black hair and big lips. The performance
shots are intercut with footage of laser shows,
silver glitter covered disco dancers, pickup trucks
(must be from Dean Arbour) and light shows at a
rave. Online music videos will be crucial to Lizzy's
later success as Lana Del Rey. In this one, she
dances sometimes hesitantly and sometimes with
abandon, usually while lip-syncing. She salutes
or points a gun to her head rhythmically. There is
footage of her getting into a car.

During certain lines, she grins childishly, raises her hand revealing overlong white fingernails and tight rings. We see cheap blinds and shiny blue streamers – the 'Blue Ribbons' she mentions in her names and the alternate title for 'Gramma' – form the backdrop. A sadness seems to come over her on the 'trampoline' line and she looks offscreen – maybe it's the nostalgia. But she's back to smiling and waving as the 'silver screen' line hits again. The video ends mid-pixellation-shudder.

Put Me in a Movie

This was on *No Kung Fu*, the demo EP she sent out which piqued the interest of David Kahne. It was originally titled 'Little Girls' and directly references *Lolita* – the character Clare Quilty is Humbert's döppelganger, who rather than loving Lolita, wants to put her in a porno. Lolita loves Quilty.

The southern US vibe is reinforced with the Spanish cue for the beginning of a take on a film set. Lizzy's vocal is restrained over booming Led Zeppelin type drums. She directly and disturbingly tries to seduce an older man, playing Lolita. There is an unusual suspended harmony on the most distressing word, underlining the tension. There are very tight rhythmic harmonies – her vocal talents are deployed to good effect here. The beginning-of-take cue gets higher and madder, and strings come in.

She puts words in Clare's mouth, referencing her previous name Sparkle Jump Rope Queen. She pleads with him for help – she could be talking about a road trip like in *Lolita*, or an artistic or personal journey. The muted chiming sounds in the background are very musical but slightly tense and, in a way, youthful.

Smarty

Lizzie loves Christmas (as explained in 'Trash Magic' and other unreleased songs), and uses it here to mean happiness (as if she is a present to be unwrapped). She talks about her trademark dress and implores her lover to be with her till the end of winter (as if she is a seasonal decoration in her dress), and then begs for him to stay forever.

She is the eponymous 'Smarty' (as she says in the unreleased 'Noir'). The spoken chorus talks about the uniqueness of her looks, her singing and her independence: the very things that characterise her as a wandering performer. The vocals are very effective in this section – she sounds solid and sure.

Although the hook is confident, this song details an abusive relationship. She nonchalantly sings about her boyfriend's psychological and physical abuse towards her, with an air only of mild annoyance. The bridge mentions how her beau in this case had been a heavy-metaller as a youth. Lizzy's connection to rock music and rockers is a running theme in her work.

The music begins with a strange twinkling descent. Almost French or Balkan accordion music comes in – the whole thing begins to sound like a twisted Christmas display. The California guitar switches up the vibe, but the overall effect here is of a mish-mash. While the music is strange, the use of spoken word in this track is extremely effective: the unhurried modulation between singing and speaking sounds amazing, not least because the speaking voice Lizzy affects, complete with low vocal fry, sounds compelling all on its own.

Yayo

Yayo means cocaine. Lana's boyfriend is a drug dealer with her favourite colour, blue, in his tattoo. This is one of the few songs on this album that is not co-written. In the modern music industry, co-writing is rampant – it's simply faster and more efficient than working with no collaborators and allows the formation of a "sound" or aesthetic to be accelerated. It's common for singers to collaborate with instrumentalists – even if they can play instruments themselves. Singers will often write the lyrics even if they surrender some of the music to their collaborators. This song will survive the transition to *Paradise*, when all the other songs will be co-writes.

She implores her biker bad boy boyfriend to take her to fabulous Las Vegas to get married. She references classic themes of relationships as addiction, and herself as a baby and the boyfriend as daddy. Her voice quavers ecstatically on the leaping intervals at the end of key lines.

The middle eight is incredible and more universal. The themes aren't as hedonistic and mad. Simple pleasures this time. The image of going through a tunnel lined with yellow lights – in the middle of a city, on the way to an airport... escapism and the road are hidden themes of this song. She wants to get married and wear his sparkle. The refrain reveals how she is ever the performer, with a strong sense of style and romance.

Born To Die

Three months after the late release of *Lana Del Ray,* containing material that she considered old and stale, Lana met new managers: Ben Mawson and Ed Millett. They bought her out of her contract with 5 Points, which had effectively stalled. *Lana Del Ray* was pulled, like *Sirens* before it. Back to square one – third time lucky.

She moved to London and moved in with Mawson. At about this time the spelling of her stage name was finalised. From now on, she would be known as Lana Del Rey. Different sources claim that she invented it, that her friends from Miami or Cuba invented it, that her management invented it...

Since the previous two LPs were pulled very quickly, for many, *Born To Die* was Lana Del Rey's "debut". Journalists and fans alike were polarised by the phenomenon coming into existence apparently fully-formed, the music industry cliché of the "overnight success" in full effect. The public and press were hit by this album with no clear warning (although of course any fan would have known what was happening).

By this point her aesthetic had solidified. In this album, her obsessions will surface in a focused manner. Nabokov's *Lolita* even gets its own song. Emily Dickinson is such a kindred spirit with Lana that there is even an online quiz juxtaposing her lines with Lana's lyrics, asking the test-taker to guess who said what.

Born To Die

This atmospheric track features *Gone With The Wind* strings, a metallic snare, breathy backing vocals and a sad, elegiac lead vocal part.

The video has Lana in daisy dukes and red Chucks making out with an all-American, tattooed bad boy on the hood of his car, interspersed with her on a throne in some sort of computer-generated palace with tigers on each side. She breathlessly quotes Lou Reed, inverting the tone of his delivery.

This song feels very final, with a deathbed- or out-of-body-like reminiscence about a confusing childhood. However, the overthinking is never exposed as baldly as when she was just Elizabeth. She sleeps with her lover's hand on her throat. The illuminated road and the headlights in the video are taken straight from her old lyrics. Back in the palace, Lana's hand motions are like Baphomet's. The song eventually reveals itself to be about the futility of love in the face of death.

The middle eight is well constructed with a recapitulation of earlier lyrics over different chords. The video finishes with her covered in blood after a car crash. It doesn't go as far as *Crash* but it definitely has a sexual element. Unlike in earlier song 'Jump', the guy survives. Brought back to life for the final shot of the video, they embrace topless in front of a rippling American flag.

As the title track, 'Born To Die' does its job of presenting some of Lana's essential themes – driving, doomed love, confusion, death – with inhuman focus and extremely expensive audio and video production, resulting in a more polished experience. The resemblance of the male protagonist of the video to Jimmy Gnecco is clear, and his rumoured connection with a car accident could have influenced the automotive carnage in the 'Born To Die' video.

Off To The Races

This track feels off-kilter, queasy, teeter-tottering on the edge of insanity – like accidentally getting way higher than you meant to.

The vocal performance is highly diverse. Lana starts with a dark low singing, changes to creepy harmonies and then becomes girlish as she rattles off the opening lines of *Lolita*. The chorus is a hiccuping affected girlish rap. Fragments of her "baby-voice" may be grating initially because the style is so developed by now but the flow works and irresistibly becomes addictive. Sometimes her vocal tones overwhelm the pitch of notes, and she almost lapses into speech.

The middle eight gets religious – she trusts in God's judgment. Combined with the religious / Catholic / Mexican B-movie parts of the video (which includes an unusual audio interpolation of Latin American library music and was pulled after negative reception but can still be found online) – so this gives the song a more tragic feel. Things get serious towards the end, where Lana touchingly states that this man is her soulmate. Upsettingly, it feels like it comes too late to make a difference to the doomed narrative.

Blue Jeans

Another iconic single from *Born To Die*, this song deals with a James Dean-esque lover who leaves Lana high and dry. The drums and verse vocals and backing vocals swagger forwards, giving the impression that they might topple over themselves. The lyrics are rap-like and the delivery of some of the verses is just as percussive and rhythmic. The production mixes the iconic lo-fi "yell" that can be heard throughout *Born To Die* with orchestral arrangements, Americana-influenced guitar sounds and her vocals, fluttering and transforming into a quacking Brooklyn whinge, or breathy, effortless ad libs.

The video is a simple black-and-white swimming pool drowning (a common trop from *Gatsby* to *Sunset Boulevard*), which goes well with the theme of doomed, unconditional, eternal love. This sentiment is twinned with the acerbic realism of her knowledge of his previous girlfriends. The vernacular she uses is her trash queen aesthetic in full swing. The video is literal – the watery blur shows us what it's like to cry forever. It ends with both of them going down. There are palm trees around, and there are alligators swimming in the pool.

She knows that he was leaving to restart his life –
note that the psychological compulsions that drive
her lovers are the same as the ones that drive her.

Video Games

'Video Games' is Lana's flagship song – the
moment when it all comes together – so I have gone
far further into its history than I have for the others.
Both the central emotion and the ultimate aesthetic
of Del Rey's canon reside here. The record company
didn't even think it was strong enough to be a
single, but when the demo was put online, it got so
many hits that they had no choice but to release it:
'Video Games' was always the one.

The languid vocals, on the edge of a drawl but
somehow still agile and on pitch, betray a quiet,
lifelong sadness. The vocals were recorded in just
a few takes and were not tuned in software. They
come straight from the source. For all the artifice
and meta-authenticity discussion that is inevitable
when one discusses Lana Del Rey, this is a real
song. The aesthetics and signifiers all build up and
orbit this moment.

She wants to make her man happy. She enjoys
the dream death inherent in end-of-the-line
relationships. The low-key drunken nights out
and sitting around, all dressed up with nowhere
to go, watching him button mash. The poignant
swelling sense of melodrama in life and in Lana's
work comes from these moments. In spite of all
the Hollywood fakery, idealisation and ideologies,
the real heart of human emotion comes from
these small meaningless moments. Playing video
games. The blueness of the dark Lana mentions is
reminiscent of the opening verse of 'Take It To The
Limit' by The Eagles.

It is difficult to understate the madness of the
production. The original song was written by
Del Rey and Justin Parker on piano, with a bit of
acoustic guitar ornamentation. The task of turning
it into a concrete track fell to production duo
Robopop. In recording and production sessions
with Lana, they slowed the tempo, adjusted the
lyrics, recorded vocals and added instrumentation.

Both members of Robopop had dual classical
and music technology backgrounds – Brandon
Lowry studied piano while Daniel Omelio's
main instrument was classical percussion, and

both were perfectly at home with using music production software rather than large recording studios. Their classical pedigree yielded the subtly aching sadness of the piano sound – despite being a virtual simulacrum of a real piano. Equally, the distant rumbling timpani, 'American Revolution'-style snare rolls, and affecting pizzicato strings are perfectly judged.

The electronic 'video game'-y arpeggiated sounds could border on overly literal and painfully naff in less skilful hands, but this time fall just on the right side of the line, becoming a kind of overdriven glittery brilliance. The duo also added 808 subkicks (virtual kick drums from the Roland TR-808 drum machine, the iconic drum machine that became the sound of hip hop on the basis of its cheapness and persists today as a signifier of cool in pop music). This fed into the hip hop crossover vibes of the other Lana tracks being put together at that time.

By the time the demo was finished, the whole thing had solidified. A mysterious distinct energy had irreversibly formed in the rough production process and couldn't be cast aside. In fact, the demo was sent to professional mix engineers, but nothing they did could trump the original. I am reminded of

Springsteen's *Nebraska*, for which all re-recording attempts came to nothing and eventually drove the sound engineer to tears. It was posted online, blew up and led to Lana signing her major label deal.

The video is just as iconic as the track itself. The grainy cut-up home video echoes Lana's early attempts to promote herself by chopping up animated Disney video and old film footage and interspersing home-video performance shots, invariably resulting in her videos frequently being taken down from YouTube on copyright infringement claims. Words flash up on the screen: Chateau Marmont. Summertime. They foreshadow lyrics in her other tracks, but it goes further than that. They help to define Lana's fantasy world. The high resolution time lapse of a rose blooming intentionally juxtaposed with the low quality sections of the video reiterate Lana's self awareness. This is manufactured. This is cut up. But when she finally reveals her false coy smile distorted through her distinctive lips, everything becomes realer than ever before. Lana has said that the aesthetic was developed partially by her photographer younger sister Caroline "Chuck" Grant.

This song is steeped in a kind of hallucinatory nostalgia, bittersweetly star-crossed and sad. The musical, visual and lyrical elements all come together and articulate something about love and life that I fail to put into words here. But it's real. The phenomenon of Lana Del Rey can be looked at in many ways. When I am at my most cynical, I see disparate audiovisual and cultural tropes assembled into a buzzword scaffolding with no emotional core. Not so with 'Video Games' – it is the song that lights up Lana's network of pop culture associations like a switchboard. It is the one.

Diet Mountain Dew

A New York fairytale about preferring the bad boy despite the unsustainability of such a relationship and the implicit conflict between that and the idea of eternal love. She compares men to alcohol or drugs as she has done in interviews (even claiming that a lot of her love songs are just about drinking). The heart sunglasses she talks about are exactly like the ones Lolita wears. She drawls about removing the Jesus statuette from the car dashboard implying that they're about to have sex, or otherwise sin, in the car. She seems less reverent towards Jesus than she was in the past.

National Anthem

Lana, in character as Jackie O, gives an interesting soliloquy by way of introducing this track's video. She makes comments about experiencing life being more important than morality, which is a viewpoint worthy of Lord Henry Wotton from *Dorian Gray.* In this track Marilyn and JFK are established as icons of Lana's world (note she had an unreleased song called 'JFK'). She is an ingénue – at the start of the song, she doesn't know how to be cool, but this changes rapidly. She instructs her lover in similar terms to those she uses in 'Video Games'.

Musically, the electronic arpeggios and military string figures combined with the rap-like patter of the verse lyrics help to establish *Born To Die*'s distinctive trip hop stylings. The chorus is a perfect fusion of her proud love of Americana and her desire to be validated by her rich, charismatic lover.

The video features A$AP Rocky as the President of the US and mixed race kids as another self-subversion, instead of having a white, older, biker boyfriend. They get down in modern hip-hop style, a cool juxtaposition with the White House surroundings.

The money-related theme of this song harks back to the short film *Poolside* which Lana starred in (as Lizzy Grant). The spiritual emptiness of wealth is well-known to her, but in this song the surface pleasures dominate.

Dark Paradise

This song is slightly more upbeat, upfront and vocally monolithic than the others. The production is trip hop, verging on industrial. Lyrically, she is Ophelia, drowning herself. The line comparing the male ex-lover's face to an unforgettable melody cuts across genres to reference 'Replay' by Iyaz.

This song is very focused and is all about an eternal doomed love that continues after the death (or final departure) of the man, and seems to be inspiring the death of the girl. The fixation with death here seems archetypal but could be to do with the numerous deaths Lana has been close to, such as her ex, K, and the friends and ex-girlfriend of Jimmy Gnecco.

Radio

Simplistic structurally and lyrically, 'Radio' fits into *Born To Die* while skirting around the normal tropes. Lyrically, it talks about what might be more standard fare in hip-hop – the artist's own success. This is the antithesis to the lo-fi indie aesthetic and makes clearer Lana's intentions to craft an aesthetic that overlaps with the hipster royalty of Pitchfork without subscribing to its ideology, thwarting the journalistic constructs of indie scene queen and then exile that were established around her by fawning journalists without her provocation, let alone consent. She sings simply of her songs getting radio airplay and gloats coolly to the old doubters.

Lana is happy to talk about herself as a singer openly – a kind of fourth-wall-breaking authenticity, as discussed in 'Mermaid Motel', which is perhaps more common in hip-hop styles (although not without precedent – Springsteen talks about the record label giving him a big advance in Rosalita, and 'playing in a band' is a trope for Bryan Adams and other American rockers). In this song she directly explains that this is the culmination of her dream. But it doesn't seem like a contradiction to

'Video Games' – more of a dream sequence where she thinks everything can be solved by success. Sadly, she already knows that this isn't true, as evidenced by songs like 'Brite Lites'.

Carmen

This song was co-written with Justin Parker of 'Video Games' and is set in Coney Island, portrayed as New York's answer to Las Vegas / Sin City. Her voice is girlish as she admonishes herself ("Put your red dress on"). Carmen is an alcoholic singer selling her body on the streets of Coney Island. The name "Carmen" literally means "song" and is taken from *Lolita*, where Lolita sings: "Oh my Carmen, my little Carmen...".

The tying of cherry knots that she mentions is an arcane behaviour where one ties a cherry stem into a knot in one's mouth – the implication being that one is good with one's tongue. The lifestyle of finding comfort and even salvation in the arms of strangers is a different way of life alluded to in 'Ride' as well. The way Carmen responds to the camera implies she's a star of some kind, but there are lines that imply she is a prostitute. "Party favours" is an old Hollywood euphemism for sexual favours on the casting couch.

The old self-made video, with flashing cameras and trashy hoop earrings, ends with Erik Satie's Gymnopédie n°1, regarded as a classical precursor to 'ambient' music and directed to be played "slow and painfully" ("lent et douloureux"). The comparison of Carmen's mind to a precious stone is from *Twin Peaks*, where the same quality is ascribed to Windom Earl, meaning his mind is brilliant, hard and cold. Lana is a noted David Lynch fan. The video also contains Lana's favourite time-lapse footage of a blooming rose alongside real or imagined microscope video of synapses and red blood cells. There is also some *Wuthering Heights*-esque doomed-love-frolicking.

Million Dollar Man

She manages to over-pronounce and yet maintain the breathiness of even her most powerful vocals, as she runs her hands over her face in her old self-made video (with her blonde locks in a different style to the professionally produced videos for the singles). The construct of the chorus is very effective. Her smile and modulation through her different voices – flutters and nasal quacks – both work fantastically together.

The chords are cinematic and sophisticated, and go well with her device of blooming flowers (this time rendered lyrically). The money-related punning fits the anachronism of her persona. Her vocals become sultrier as the song progresses.

In the song, her lover is unbearably handsome and rich. The lyrics reference Elvis's 'Blue Suede Shoes'. She loves her man's flaws, and she loves that he sees her as unique.

In early live versions she would sing a slightly different chorus, changing the meaning from "I'm ready to go with you" to "I'm ready to leave you". This calls to mind a badgering boyfriend asking if she's ok, or why she seems detached, when it's already too late – she's already made her mind up to leave him. However the final cut of the song doesn't have this meaning and leaves the question of why their relationship is in its death throes open to interpretation.

Her voice is fantastic on this track, shooting up into her higher registers. It conveys both power and admiring disbelief. In the video she seems to know it too – she's beaming.

Summertime Sadness

The video shows her with a lesbian lover – subverting the bad boyfriend meme that has run through much of her work. Her red party dress trope reappears here. She alludes to Springsteen's 'Dancing In The Dark'. Electricity and annihilation feature in the burning telephone wires. The melody in the middle eight is effortlessly emotionally piercing with a saddening image of how natural forces keep the stars and the morning sun apart.

The Cedric Gervais remix of the song was a runaway success, becoming a sleeper hit and expanding Lana's audience to Gervais' more EDM-oriented fanbase. The track got extended longevity and the sadness was pumped up into something frenzied and hysterical which could be equally at home at student cheese nights full of skinny jeans or proper gurning, frothing-at-the-mouth raves.

This Is What Makes Us Girls

This track has an atmospheric, nostalgic feel.
Pabst Blue Ribbon is a hipness signifier from
Lynch's *Blue Velvet*, but blue ribbons have a literal
meaning for her, as we know. She lays the imagery
on thick as she talks about eye makeup, which also
obliquely references her YouTube aesthetic, which
included illegally spliced Disney footage.

Lana is more conversational in this track. There's
a kind of sincerity, even if it's a bit goofy, that
isn't present in the other songs on this album,
and the production is aggressive to compensate.
The crashing snare sounds like 'Total Eclipse Of
The Heart'. Some lines are noticeably more down
to earth in the context of this album, although
for earlier phases of her career they would seem
normal.

In the middle eight she reminisces about the girls'
attractiveness, youth and social capital – the zenith
for people who peak in high school. This song
immortalises how a young Lana was sent by her
parents to a boarding school in Connecticut to stop
her drinking.

Without You

In this song Lana talks about how fame pales in comparison to love. His love is a health hazard, and she wants to be his fragile, perfect doll. When she talks about the unintended negative space of the American Dream, it's very Springsteen-esque but also sums up her whole M.O. for this album. The music sounds like a ticking clock at the start – there's something of a child's music box about it. The appropriated visuals she talks about could be referring to the way her reality and fantasy start to blur now that she's totally immersed in the world of tropes and clichés. It could also refer to the *saudade* (Portuguese for, roughly, "nostalgia for a time that never existed") of having experienced many lives through consumption of pop-cultural myths. Finally, it could be a literal reference to the way she would illegally splice together copyrighted footage to make her YouTube music videos.

It took Taylor Swift until 2015's 'Wildest Dreams' to try to knock off the chorus vibe of this (2012) song, which fans quickly noticed. Check out the YouTube video entitled 'Lana Del Rey – Without You (live)' for one of Lana's most emotional performances.

Lolita

This track gets straight to the point, firing the mental shotgun of all the associations of Nabokov's *Lolita*, connotations lighting up even in the minds of those who have never read the book.

The song was written with Liam Howe and prototyped as a bright 60s American surf pop piece, which can be seen alongside the original video online with Lana smiling coyly with bleach blonde hair. Clips of Japanese girl squads powering up contribute to the characterisation of her as a child, although she appears to be a woman.

The song was reworked into the more trip hop style of the whole album and, to me, has the most assertive production on *Born To Die*. The delayed and chopped vocals in the middle eight are both childish, like a toddler asking "are we there yet?", and sinister, like the beating of the tell-tale heart. The strings survive from the original demo but the surf guitar is gone and replaced with crashing single stabs like a kind of twisted motown. Her declaration of independent single-mindedness is spoken, not sung, to deeply sinister effect.

In this Lana plays the temptress again, and the theme of younger girls with older men is brought into uncomfortably sharp relief, the likes of which we have not seen since 'Put Me In A Movie'.

The prosody between the music and the lyrics is excellent – the chanted letters and her girlish, nasal, hellish whine interact synergistically to create a disturbing implication of playground immaturity and undertones of premature sexuality. The namechecked Romeo is not only a forbidden lover, but in the modern consciousness, *Romeo & Juliet* is about young – technically underage – love.

Stanley Kubrick directed a version of *Lolita* but there is no special reference to it here. However there is a Kubrickian undercurrent to Lana's work. She had an unreleased track called 'Strangelove', her next album will be called *Ultraviolence* and she would definitely be up for meeting the Star Child at the end of *2001: A Space Odyssey* given her spacey themes in 'Oh Say Can You See'.

Lucky Ones

This track is about the joy of escaping a dead end town with a lover (the kind that Adele's ex may not have escaped in 'Hello').

The initial rhymes are straight out of 'I'm On Fire' by Bruce Springsteen, which has a video that could easily be in Lana's universe: a rich married woman who lives out in The Hills drops her car off at the garage where The Boss is a mechanic. He drives it out to her and thinks of ringing the doorbell, but then drives it back to the garage so she can collect it and is none the wiser about his infatuation. In Lana's world, the genders are inverted.

Getting into the car and leaving a town full of losers is again a Springsteen reference, this time to 'Born To Run'. Lana compares herself to a child again at times. She talks about an overriding plan for life or the universe, which borders on religious. Her positive characterisation of craziness shows her coming to terms with her unique madness which in the past she has tried to deny or hide. In this way this track is actually less saccharine than a happy love song could be.

Paradise

Ride

The 'Ride' video begins and ends with melodramatic soliloquies that only hold together when spoken in her voice, backed by swooning strings. She establishes a backstory where she's a wandering singer, taking up with any guy who will pick her up. She gives a perpetually sad confused look but comes alive on stage. She wraps herself in an American flag, and is seen biking across the desert with Hell's Angels.

She swings on a massive tyre swing in the desert – openly nonsensical and surreal. She sadly says she was destined to always be the side chick. The monologues provoked a polar response – cringe or moving. Too earnest, it made listeners in the US, Switzerland, Ireland and France balk, causing the song to only be a minor hit in those countries. However, in Russia and Belgium, it reached the top 10.

Her vocals are extremely expressive. The emotion and prosody of the melody of the main song are affecting. Her emotional scream of exhaustion at feeling insane punches through the affectations. She talks about her figurative old man as white and gold, or the white hair of a once-blonde man. She nostalgically talks about her actual father. She liquefies the line between her life and her persona.

American

Lana starts by referencing 'Baby, Let's Play House' by Elvis. She immediately and directly establishes the massive influence of Springsteen and Elvis in dialogue within the lyrics. The admiration of her lover's tanned skin is straight out of 'Boys Of Summer' by Don Henley.

She uses slang like a bratty teen to breathe a bit of modernity into what would otherwise be a fully retro aesthetic. The vocal reverb in the chorus is euphoric and has been calibrated to perfection. Again she infantilises herself.

The chorus and wordless post-chorus oohs sound fondly nostalgic. She seems to have developed a fondness for LA by now as well. She's aware that sometimes she is disingenuous, and in this song she prays.

Cola

The demo title of this song was 'Pussy'. Even with the title change, the first line brings it back – 'my pussy tastes like pepsi-cola', reportedly taken from her ex-boyfriend Barrie-James O'Neill's impression of his version of a typical American girl.

Lana's eyes are wide because she's in love or high. Lolita drank Coke, as did Lana Turner when she was getting discovered by showbiz moguls. This song talks about her liking older men. Her use of pet names isn't arbitrary – *Pretty Baby* (1978) features a 12-year-old prostitute – in turn inspired by the song 'Pretty Baby' by Tony Jackson. Lana is the other woman in this scenario – the man she's after is married.

The bridge is somehow both swaggering and infantile, including what could be a sexual innuendo regarding him decorating her neck with a necklace. It culminates in a thrilling high note. The pulse of the track is hypnotic. The outro includes recapitulations and slight variations of the ad libs at the end of the middle eight, and the killer first line, and even a tiny guitar solo. It really kicks off as it fades out, giving that sad impression of a band that plays forever, like The Killers playing 'Exitlude', the closing track of *Sam's Town*, at the end of their film *Live From The Royal Albert Hall*.

Body Electric

'I Sing the Body Electric' is a poem by Walt Whitman, from his *Leaves of Grass*. It inspired a short story collection of the same name by Ray Bradbury (which in turn inspired a television movie *The Electric Grandmother*) and which formed Bradbury's only successful script for *The Twilight Zone*. The poem is in essence a celebration of physical youth, just like this song.

Lana quickly establishes her preferred pop-cultural ancestors namedropping Elvis, Marilyn and Jesus. She name-checks the Grand Ole Opry, a venue in Nashville where Elvis played. In the second verse she mentions Whitman (of whom she has a tattoo, along with Nabokov) directly.

Praying the rosary is Catholic. Mary prays for her unhinged mind. By the end of the song Mary is dancing too. In the chorus she sneaks in 'I'm On Fire' by Bruce Springsteen again. The chorus strengthens into an exaltation. This track is the intermixing of the religious, pantheistic and electric and is the first of the three songs in Lana's short film *Tropico*.

Blue Velvet

A jazz song originally performed by Tony Bennett.
Covering this lends some weight to her stylings
as a jazz singer, a mantle she will take on more
definitively in *Ultraviolence*.

She's a big David Lynch fan – his film *Blue Velvet*
is related to this song by its name and its theme of
violence, with lovers calling each other mommy and
daddy during domestic abuse.

The video was an H&M advert in 2012. It is strange
but everyone in it is impeccably styled – the sailor,
the hypnotist, the soldier and the three Lana clones.
Lana herself wears a strangely fuzzy sweater on
stage. A small person comes in and turns off the
record provoking laughter. Lana smiles awkwardly.
The advert manages to inject a bit of humour into a
serious, almost melodramatic cover.

Gods & Monsters

She is shown in *Day Of The Dead*-style makeup
with Shaun. She appropriates chola style and has a
double teardrop tattoo meaning she has committed
murder or been raped in prison (it depends). She

hangs with gangsters and pole dances. She talks about falling out with God (this is fleshed out in *Tropico* where she plays Eve). She idolises Jim Morrison's fast living, which ended with a heroin overdose. The "hotel sprees" and "innocence lost" are *Lolita*-esque (Lolita loses her virginity in a motel room).

Lana blurs the line between a groupie and a real singer, a comment on her lifestyle which reflects the wider truth of content creation and consumption in an age where professional sounding tracks are made in bedrooms and home studios (see 'Video Games').

"Life imitates art", hackneyed by overuse, is an Oscar Wilde quotation. He is as good a role model as any for her. Her sex-talk-like definition of heaven integrates her existential and religious pondering with physical pleasures in a Whitmanesque fashion.

This is the second song in *Tropico* and was covered for *American Horror Story: Freak Show*, which shares aspects of Lana's violently kitsch aesthetic.

Yayo

See *Lizzy Grant a.k.a. Lana Del Ray*

Bel Air

From *Born To Die – The Paradise Edition*, the last of the three songs featured in Lana's short film *Tropico*. In this third section, which features as the music video to 'Bel Air', Adam and Eve ascend to heaven aided by flying saucers. *Tropico* stars Lana as the Biblical Eve and Shaun Ross (the first male albino model – he is actually of African-American descent but has white skin) as Adam. Lana also stars as Mary Magdalene.

The original video featured her standing in a smoky room but was taken down. It is typical for Lana's camp to redact and take down material no longer deemed relevant, to ensure purity of the message.

She talks about resurrection (which in *Tropico* is literal, with her baptism). The lover seems an unattainable bad boy in this song. She promises that she won't play him anymore, but he's already gone. It sounds almost funereal.

The song sidesteps the potential cultural crossed wires with the famous *Fresh Prince of Bel-Air* by being a rather serious affair of piano and strings, "classy" signifiers. In message, it's like a retro version of 'The Hills' by The Weeknd. Roses, Bel Air and palm trees are all symbolic shortcuts to the place she wants to go.

The melody is plunging, sad and reaches out in desperation. The song references 'Sweet Child O' Mine' by Guns 'N' Roses by name (she has a song named after the band as well).

Burning Desire

The weird synth/electric piano plucks that cut through the intro strings are reminiscent of those in 'Ashes to Ashes' by David Bowie. There's a cool heavy breathing effect, and the opening melody and chords sound similar to Mark Lanegan's 'When Your Number Isn't Up'.

Lana's vocals are breathy and sensual. She reminds us she's driven everywhere. Her agitated whispering gives the track its emotional dimension.

The song is also about speeding in a car, tinging the whole thing with fear. In the video she's alone on the stage, dancing a bit, intercut with footage of driving and blooming flowers. The hall seems to be empty. The suggestive breathing is recapitulated towards the end.

The vocal expertise is standout here. The breathless harmonies in the middle eight have a beautiful chiming quality.

Strangely this song was the title track to a 13-minute advert *Desire* for the Jaguar F-type in 2013 produced by Ridley Scott, starring Damian Lewis as a hapless suited and booted Jaguar car delivery man who gets embroiled in a goofy and unlikely gangster caper.

Tropico

Tropico is a short film and EP of the same name containing 'Body Electric', 'Gods and Monsters' and 'Bel Air'. The film is split into three sections corresponding with the songs. It really must be seen to be believed.

In the first section, Lana plays Eve and bites the apple. In the Garden of Eden, we also find Elvis and Marilyn. In the second section, Lana starts to recite Whitman's 'I Sing The Body Electric', and is then shown with her Adam in modern LA (she's now a stripper and he's a gang member). Lana recites a bit of 'Howl'. In the last section, God recites a bit of John Mitchum's 'Why I Love America' before Adam and Eve ascend to Heaven surrounded by flying saucers.

The film travels through different notions of mythic America – different sectors of Lana's universe – and brings Lana's love of poetry to the fore.

Ultraviolence

The title acknowledges Lana's latent Kubrick influence and happily commemorates Lana having the same name for two LPs in a row. This is a stripped down, more focused album than *Born To Die* and delves back into Lana's past. The album was recorded and produced by Dan Auerbach of The Black Keys, at his studio. The increased references to rock and heavy metal (favourites of Lana), especially in relation to a male lover, seem to place Jimmy Gnecco at the heart of this album.

Cruel World

The opening track of *Ultraviolence* and Lana's favourite on the album, this song talks about a relationship that ended, allowing her to finally be happy. But she talks about how they they remain crazy – for each other. That's what makes it a cruel world. But she's happy now. She puts her iconic little red party dress on, gets Bourbon and "suburban" – brilliant. An echo of the suburban boredom of 'Video Games'. Her ex was a religious gun-toting party animal as usual but this time she's glad to be rid of him. She talks about how she found a rebound to get over him.

Ultraviolence

Another classic Lana construction, the title alludes to the drug-fuelled depraved antics of Alex and his droogs in *Clockwork Orange,* which include rape and murder. Likewise this song's killer line is pinched from the Carole King/Gerry Goffin song of the same name. Sung by The Crystals, it dealt with a real case of domestic abuse. King's babysitter Little Eva was being beaten by her boyfriend. When asked why she didn't leave him, she replied that the abuse was motivated by love. Carole King, who had survived domestic abuse herself, later expressed regret about having had anything to do with the song.

King claims that she first uttered the famous line herself although it can be traced back to the Hungarian play by Ferenc Molnàr which inspired the 1930 film *Liliom* by Frank Borzage. and the Rodgers and Hammerstein musical *Carousel*, which spawned a 1956 film *Carousel* which may have been subconsciously plagiarised by contemporaries (like George Harrison having done so to create 'My Sweet Lord' from 'He's So Fine' by Ronnie Mack, performed by The Chiffons).

Lana's re-contextualisation of the title and this killer line are exemplars of her mastery of the pop culture trope. She co-opts them to create something new and original while harnessing the efficiency of cultural connotations. She barely has to say a thing. Prior to this album, Lana's boyfriend(s) have been described as bad men who like bad girls. Now, the stakes are upped as physical violence is the name of the game.

The lyric is replete with double meanings – sirens both signifying the law, and the class of seductresses which Lana herself belongs to. It's also harking back to *Sirens* the album (and 'Sirens' the song) by her previous incarnation May Jailer, in which her ex-lover and friend K dies. She communicates her fear of death at the hands of her abuser in a way that could equally mean she felt so happy she could die.

The backing vocals towards the end foreshadow upcoming song 'Fucked My Way Up To The Top'. Loving pain is the theme. The sirens and violins that she hears in the chorus could be the ringing in her ears after a blow to the head. Or her own melodramatic fantasy overwhelming her. We are welcomed to the middle eight by tears of lemonade, an infantile symbol for sweet tears. The "white lines" in the song are most obviously cocaine but could be self-harm scars.

The video features Lana as a jilted bride – or maybe the fiancé didn't live long enough to make the wedding? Her boyfriend Barrie-James O'Neill could be "Jim", as could alleged ex-boyfriend Jimmy Gnecco (they could have been engaged – Brite Lites' Lana takes off what she calls her wedding ring), or icon Jim Morrison (which would explain the Woodstock stuff and the lone-bride video). The use of the name "Jim" with the lyric talking about cults suggests Jim Jones, who will be played by Father John Misty and thus directly referenced in the music video for 'Freak' on *Honeymoon*.

Lana talks about how her love just wasn't enough for Jim, harking back to 'Born To Die', which talks about how sometimes life just gets in the way of love. It's a dash of realism in a predominantly mythic universe.

Shades Of Cool

The chorus is iridescent, featuring both her high open tone and slightly breathy low voice. The way the strings and voice trade licks is highly musical. The carefully regulated "wah wah" guitar adds colour without getting in the way, although it threatens to become corny (like any opinionated bit of musical arrangement).

During the guitar solo a more corporeal Lana is dancing, drinking, swimming, eating strawberries... she puts her arms around him. She loves him. The song's way of talking about mercurial, possibly violent moods through the weather is a reference to Marianne Faithfull's song 'Strange Weather' – which actually seems to have influenced the overall sound of this song.

The video is full of oversaturated colours like the LA-based *Drive* by Nicolas Winding Refn. Her old man drives across the city. Lana appears as a ghostly vision. Her voice in the outro, and the sudden impact of a minor chord with the jazzy cymbal roll is beautiful. At the corresponding point in the video, her old man is driving away intercut with scenes of them dancing. But Lana pulls away and falls to the floor, still laughing, undiminished.

Brooklyn Baby

This song is an ambiguously ironic parody of a hipster queen, co-written with then-boyfriend Barrie James O'Neill. She exaggerates the indie darling tropes until they become almost ridiculous (consider the low voice that comes in towards the end of the song). The "cooler-than-thou" attitude is realistically aggravating. It starts off ambiguously as self-assurance and soon blows the lid off, explicitly asserting her own cool-dominance over her boyfriend. She's talking about her generation, like The Who.

The moment of sincerity in the middle eight is welcome – it's a well-executed statement of exasperation. It works well as a musical contrast, and lyrically expresses the impasse of trying to make an outsider understand your lifestyle. Lana's love of Brooklyn, her home for many years, is well-known.

West Coast

The topline references 'Edge Of Seventeen' by Stevie Nicks, while the music sometimes sounds Beatles-esque. The emotion of the vocal is effortless and breathy, reflecting the uncomfortable collision of Lana's career aspirations (and maybe her dreams of future experiences in general) and her current relationship. Here California is the land of opportunity.

The musical foundation drops out from beneath us with a jolting tempo decrease in the chorus. It's not clear whether she loves him or not, but she's moving on either way, just like in all her other songs on this topic.

Sad Girl

Lana talks more frankly about being the other woman here. She wallows unapologetically in her sadness which for journalist Lindsay Zoladz, is a feminist move – a woman reclaiming her emotions from a patriarchy that would have her ever-smiling to satisfy the male gaze. Bonny, aside from its normal meaning, could reference the commit-crimes-and-bang of Bonnie and Clyde. This calls to mind Brigitte Bardot and Serge Gainsbourg's 'Bonnie & Clyde'.

In light of 'National Anthem', one cannot help but feel there is something Lewinsky-esque about it. 'I'm On Fire' is one of her stock Springsteen allusions. She reiterates that she's a bad girl. As the production on this album leans towards slow atmospheric rock, the hip-hop lyrical signifiers are intensified to compensate.

Pretty When You Cry

This song was improvised and recorded in one take. That's why you can hear breaks in the voice and strange quirks in the dynamics. She sounds vulnerable and needy. She laments how he never manages to get it done. She can't compete with his substance abuse habits. The prechorus is a nice change of pace.

Her voice gets pinched and sad, going higher and higher, and a messy, vibey guitar solo starts cutting through the track. The intriguing killer line in this song explains how she's stronger than every one of her boyfriends apart from this one.

Money Power Glory

In this song the more manipulative element to Lana, hinted at in 'Lolita', is explored further. She wants to take him for all that he's got. She's a hustler now, and her image of a street-walking singer is no longer as submissive. She states in no uncertain terms that she's a bad girl, and dope 'n' diamonds are familiar territory. The melody is stratospheric, a chorus of double tracked fallen angels. God / Hallelujah bring the Catholic glory back to this track. The sun also rises is from the Bible, via the eponymous novel by Hemingway: Brett won't grow her hair and fails to heed society's call like Lana does in this song.

Fucked My Way Up To The Top

This song is an ironic take on accusations levelled at Lana by the music press and internet trolls alike. She has talked in interviews about her romantic relationships with men in the music industry, and how none of them has advanced her career. In the song, she is unapologetic and positive, and her voice is exultant. This track functions, on one level, as an unlikely love song.

However, Lana has commented in *Grazia* that the song is about an unnamed female singer who first criticised Lana for being inauthentic and then appropriated Lana's style for herself. This would change the lyrical stabs at the other woman from expressions of jealousy over a man / some men into more direct "diss-track" fare. In a way, this is as much a hip-hop signifier as Lana's various uses of slang and beats: rappers' "beefs" are a well-known part of their personas.

Old Money

This song is in the same mould as 'Bel Air'. She's going back to her man – her nostalgia is overwhelming. This song is melodically indebted to Nino Rota's 'What Is a Youth' (or 'Love Theme From Romeo and Juliet' for Franco Zeffirelli's 1968 film *Romeo and Juliet*).

Blue hydrangeas and red white and blue items are taken from her old song 'Axl Rose Husband' from her Sparkle Jump Rope Queen MySpace. This shows how long it takes for some ideas to come to fruition. Sunset and Vine means the intersection of Vine Street and Sunset Boulevard in LA, but is also reminiscent Tom Waits' album *Heartattack And Vine*. Tom Waits is another character in the Laurel Canyon scene, and was also a barfly, eternal nomad and fully self-actualised persona like Lana.

Fitting into *The Great Gatsby* world via 'Young And Beautiful', she asks if her lover will still love her when she is still good with rhymes but after her looks have faded. She's no longer the 'Brooklyn Baby'. One of the monosyllabic refrains sounds very sexual and fits in with the physical pleasure signifiers.

A slightly different reading interprets this song to be about a guy from her past that she still loves and wants to go back to. The sensual physical pleasures are all things that they did or had when they were together. Another possible interpretation is that this is actually about her parents. Her father became rich within his lifetime (which was a secondary factor in the backlash against her initial success). She's talking about her own youth, which could bring her parents into the picture.

The Other Woman

This is Lana's first Nina Simone cover (the second being 'Don't Let Me Be Misunderstood'). She mentions the title in the opening monologue to 'Ride'. Lana is a big fan of Nina and has her tattooed on her collarbone, as one of the travelling singers and writers she likes to take on the road with her.

The song is fairly bleak. Lana inhabits the role of the solitary queen, always appearing glamorous, smelling and looking great, fairly easily. The final lines about the inevitability of eternal loneliness are a real kick in the teeth though – Lana hasn't spoken about this as directly in her own lyrics. The production blends this track flawlessly with the originals on *Ultraviolence*. Lana's fluttering, quavering ad libs at the end before the final "alone" are arresting and heartbreaking.

Black Beauty

"Black Beauties" are amphetamine pills – the nickname was used by truckers in the late 60s and 70s, who would take amphetemines in order to stay awake at the wheel, an idea that evokes images of long all-American drives. The song is a stripped down and raw address to her hopelessly depressive lover. Each breath is audible and the piano is soft and watery, even as the strings come in. Her voice is nonetheless plucky. The blue sparrow pet name may be related to the sailor tattoo.

Her desire to conform to his expectations goes down to the colours she adorns herself with. She wishes she was Spanish – with a name like Del Rey, of course, she could be. The chorus is majestic and moving. He is dark but beautiful. He is equated with a drug, of course. The middle eight has a pleasing parallel harmony.

This song captures the essence of a relationship doomed by her boyfriend's inherent anhedonia. Although Lana loves him completely, she is at a loss and ruefully lays her feelings bare in this moving song. The big hit of the first chorus is a standout moment in her work.

Guns and Roses

Lana co-produced this track. She talks about her hard rock lover, reminiscing about how much he loved the band Guns 'N' Roses, although her rendering of the title straightens it out to possibly be literal. In the middle eight, via a pleasingly ornate melody, she remembers how good he was at seducing her.

She muses how maybe she should have married this man, even though it wasn't going anywhere.

In light of the heavy metal references and the lyric concerning a wedding ring in 'Brite Lites', this song seems to be one of many about Jimmy Gnecco, and supports the theory that they were engaged. She had a song called 'Axl Rose Husband' on her MySpace back when she was known as Sparkle Jump Rope Queen, which is clearly connected to this song via Guns 'N' Roses and the concept of marriage.

Florida Kilos

Intriguingly, this song was co-written with Harmony Korine, best known as the writer of *Kids* and the director of *Gummo* and *Spring Breakers*. *Kids* is a work of hysterical realism and portrait of the lives of young people in Manhattan during the AIDS crisis. *Spring Breakers* is full of good girls gone bad who meet and start rolling with a drug dealer played by James Franco. Incidentally Franco has since taken an interest.

The refrain is a later use of that street name for cocaine than her song 'Yayo' but cuts to the heart of the subject of this song – the Miami coke dealer scene. Lana has said she loves the idea of mastering something regardless of its legality.

However she comes across as young and naive in the opening lines. The passion she feels in this song is so strong that she doesn't mind being incarcerated as long as it's in the name of this love. The very final line echoes a melody from 'Dark Paradise' on *Born To Die*.

Lana once summed up *Born To Die* as "Bruce Springsteen in Miami", and here she arrives but as more of an ingenue character. The concept of an anonymous, insane "Florida man" has become an internet meme resulting from the availability of Florida police records of the drug-addled antics of crazy men in Florida, and has inspired a film of the same name, making Florida seem like a nexus for the marginalised.

The production is expansive compared to *Ultraviolence*'s overriding restraint, featuring creative use of echoes, reverbs, harmonies and swelling electronic section-transition sounds.

Is This Happiness

The piano has a clearer sound than usual, whereas Lana's voice is almost being swallowed by her own accent and reverb. A bit of birdsong at the start of the second verse harks back to the avian themes of *Sirens*, and other ambient sounds break up the more conventional production.

The chorus is a direct question, a simple refrain of the title. Lyrically one is reminded of 'Is This It', the opening track of *Is This It* by The Strokes. The purple pills sound like morphine. There is a telling reference to Hunter S Thompson – Lana's own work is slightly gonzo and seems to involve drugs. She sounds sad and weary about her lover's inability to control his anger, and hopes her father will defend her from any potential trigger-happy tantrum of his.

The mentions of Hollywood and stars may mean this is a reference to when Jimmy Gnecco left to pursue his career, as in 'Blue Jeans'. The middle eight is interesting and slightly new-age-y in its reference to witch hazel. Here Lana sneeringly references Hunter S Thompson again, alluding to his suicide method.

Flipside

'Flipside' is a bonus track on *Ultraviolence*. This song deals with losing a love and a kind of dual denial – she speculates that maybe they could get back together again – and equivalent resignation in the tone. She thinks she doesn't want to hurt him but the relationship is fizzling. He seduced her once, and she wonders if he can do it again – that is, whether the relationship can be revitalised or not.

He appears to be a famous singer – she's getting dressed up to go and hear him. She namechecks one of her favourites, Springsteen. The melody and chords are strangely happy and almost Britpoppy, and the guitar chords are straight. This song has a rocky feel with a Beatles-esque chord progression, putting it in the 60s part of Lana's world.

Honeymoon

Honeymoon

The arrangement of this song – mostly strings, percussion only entering very late – is orchestral and filmic. The sentiment of the lyric is more romantic than her usual fare. She calls this her favourite song of the album. On YouTube, there is a short video intro before a lyric sheet is shown. There's filtered footage of Lana looking pensive lying on the grass – but it's near a road.

The song is in free time, not "clicked" to a metronome. It features her favourite colour again: dark blue, which also comes up in 'Video Games'. The rich harmonies of disconnected fragments of the topline break the anachronism illusion, sounding fresh. The strings are *Gone With The Wind*-esque again, with chords that ascend and then sadly step back down. It never quite breaks away from the overriding melancholia.

Music To Watch Boys To

Lana's attitude here has elements of both submissive deference and dominating objectification. The style and melody of the backing vocals puts this song next to 'This Is What Makes Us Girls' from *Born To Die*, and some of the lyrics are taken straight from it. Some of the intentionally childish lyrics sound like 'Lolita'. The exotic-sounding synth flute adds a woozy, unexpected sound to the palette. She sums up her relationship with boys thus: she lives to love them, but her love kills them.

The video is directed by Kinga Burza, a Polish-Australian music video director – she says that Lana supplied a detailed concept which involved matching images to specific lyrics. Apparently the music Lana is listening to while gramophones rotate around her is "soft grunge".

    In Burza's words, "It wasn't one type of guy, it could have been anyone. They're being watched, but they don't realise it. It's voyeuristic ... The video epitomises everything she's into: underwater footage, Super 8 footage, a projector, the cut in between a non-linear narrative. It's the essence of her." In the video, the watery drowning references

Ophelia from *Hamlet*. The video features her playing guitar – a classic signifier of authenticity in pop music. A cinematic, overly literal music video is redeemed by the sheer quality of some of the shots.

Terrence Loves You

The initial piano chords that overtake the guitar plucks are majestic, and the vocals cut to the point; the lyrics are clearer than usual. Lana laments the loss of a musician lover. The saxophone stabs risk naff-ness but as usual come down on the right side.

She lyrically references jazz and blues, and talks about Barrie-James O'Neill, also a musician. The Terrence named in the title is David Bowie's half brother, Terrence Burns, who Bowie credits with getting him into jazz. Terrence developed schizophrenia and eventually (possibly accidentally) killed himself. The song contains an interpolation of Bowie's 'Space Oddity' in the middle eight.

The name Terrence by chance also brings to mind Terrence Mallick and *Badlands*, which was a big inspiration for Springsteen.

God Knows I Tried

The Eagles and Don Henley's 'Boys of Summer'
are known inspirations to Lana. In this track she
brings this Laurel Canyon influence to the surface.
She namechecks 'Hotel California' and 'Tequila
Sunrise' in the first verse. The chorus melody is
an homage to the tune of 'Doolin' Dalton' by the
Eagles, and overall this lover's lament has the
aching and hyperreal Californian sadness of the
Eagles' most maudlin tunes.

In this song, Lana talks about wearing her
sunglasses even when it's raining and generally
being imprisoned, violated and battered by fame.
In the song she seems to make her peace with the
fact that she will constantly be getting emotionally
killed and having to resurrect herself, now that
people attack her on a personal level as a result
of her artistic output. The chorus and bridge are
religious, and have the sound of someone coming
to terms with not being able to control everything in
life.

High By The Beach

In the video for this song Lana blows up a paparazzi

helicopter, suggesting it's about escaping from media pressure, although it clearly talks about a romantic relationship too. The lyrics really show us that Lana knows to never believe her own hype. She has spoken in interviews of how her fame never had any positive aspects – the press have never been kind to her.

Aside from the media escape narrative, the vibe of this track on *Honeymoon* is nostalgic summer indolence. The music of this song unexpectedly harks back to the production of *Born To Die*, reminding us of her ascent to fame. The 808s and beeps, with trap hi hats, are a step forward. The lazy vocals sing about re-asserting independence. A kind of reverse 'Video Games': financial independence, rejection of the dogma of a relationship... in the video she is alone. The badness of the male character doesn't validate his masculinity this time.

Her vengefulness gets her free of a bad situation. This song is comparable to 'Marina Del Rey' by George Strait, which has the lovelorn theme of some of Lana's other songs, but has the same physical setting as this one.

The video director Jake Nava says Lana wanted the video to be "Château Marmont chic". Regarding the process in general, he says she "weighs in" and has a "good sense of her own identity". Her blowing up the press helicopter is tonally typical of her post-fame videos: sincere, literal and melodramatic.

Freak

Lana's nasal hum is taken to the next level. She uses the pleasing image of a blue flame. Another perfect moment of love for Lana that struggles to exist in the continuum. An angel of flame – she's rising up from Hollywood Hell.

The trap cymbals come in and bring us back to the present day. Her dismissal of his privacy is a flash of meta self-awareness. The high notes have good moments of prosody. She's trying to snare a man into her celebrity California lifestyle.

The middle eight shifts into a romantic, slushy chord progression, with harmonies stacking up. She laments his coldness, she doesn't want to fight... reality sets in. They are fighting. Celebrities are freaks. In a musically well-founded move, the outro recapitulates her surreal humming, more full-bodied this time – the events of the song have changed nothing.

In the video, Father John Misty (Joshua Tillman, previously an artist under the name J Tillman and drummer for Fleet Foxes) plays a version of Jim Jones, cult leader who poisoned his cult in the famous Kool-Aid Jonestown murder-suicide. Lana is a member of the cult. Misty is shown taking LSD. The video has a second act which is a reprise of the under shots from the 'Music To Watch Boys To' video, including Lana's sister Chuck among other girls.

Art Deco

The filtered, gliding synths are sad, accompanying restrained, reflective vocals even as she sings about wildness. The attitude is throwaway: she characterises parties as harmless. There is a good one-word backing vocal sampled from 'Born to Die'. The use of gunmetal as a visual reference gives a stylish but latently violent feel.

The subject of this song is a young New Yorker who has been rejected by the mainstream, like Lana. The reference to 'Rapper's Delight' by Sugarhill Gang implies that Lana thinks the subject is a potential game-changer. It's not clear who the subject actually is – it could be a kind of detached self-assessment or synthesis like 'Carmen'.

Burnt Norton (Interlude)

Lana recites a short part of the start of the T.S. Eliot poem 'Burnt Norton', over a part-shoegaze, part-vaporwave instrumental. As part of the release promotion for *Honeymoon*, fans could call a mobile phone number shown on her Instagram account and would be greeted with this track.

The part of the text that remains after her brutal truncation deals with the futility of regretting or wondering what could have been. The poem later becomes more Christian and deals with the garden of the Burnt Norton house, which burned down, killing its owner.

Religion

Here Lana talks about submitting to a belief system. The chips will fall where they may – she is giving up on trying to control the outcome and instead just allowing love. She finds religion and refutes the money, drugs, parties and clubs.

She is devoted to this man. While Christian imagery has been a theme of her work, here it manifests itself directly but in a different and sacrilegious way. The reference to listening to 'Lay Lady Lay' by Dylan on repeat suggests that they just want to have sex. The image of Lana down on her knees, in the context of a romantic relationship, is suggestive. The straight shuffling drum machine is hypnotic. There's a word which sounds very similar to "pray" but isn't – a subtle and pleasing bit of wordplay.

It's slow burning and woozy. There isn't the mad tinge of tension and insanity that comes with religious repression or needing Jesus – instead Lana is a convert: she has fully gone to the other side. The song ends on a disturbing, elegant slow down to nothing.

Salvatore

An Italian sounding song, described by her as filmic and old-world Italian. Her love of certain colours shines through in her initial description of Miami. Italian American also has a connotation with New York. The Italian word in the chorus means hunter. She is a master of triggering keyword responses: the chorus is just a few words interspersed with a wordless melodious run.

The lover raps and beatboxes, bringing us back into the present day. She admits she was wrong to neglect to tell him, or the world, that she loved him – to "go public".

She enjoys her soft ice cream while Salvatore waits. The ice cream is a summer fling, but it also conjures up visions of *Lolita*. Lana makes full use of the ambiguity of the well-known Italian greeting, which crucially can mean either "hello" or "goodbye". Incidentally, "Salvatore" means saviour.

Despite the Italian vibe, Medellin is in Spain (or in drug-fuelled Latin America): she's on a kind of pan-European trip, but it holds together somehow. In the spirit of her universe, while specifics *are* important, it's still more about that melancholy feeling than the exact details.

The Blackest Day

In this song, Lana explicitly states that blue is the colour, although later it gets black. A punchy drum machine snare, different to the others, is welcome here, cutting through a dark mix. Musically, the chorus is a wonderful sliding construction, with a long delay effect on the vocal. Lana talks about her love of Billie Holiday.

While ostensibly a torch song, in many ways this is a very modern song for Lana. While all her songs make some kind of concession to modern production, with electronic instruments and hyperreal drums and vocal atmospheres, here the song is definitely structurally closer to will.i.am than Elvis. The chorus is followed by a post-chorus. This keeps modern songs, usually electronically repetitive, sounding fresh and engaging. When the pattern changes after the last chorus, the song is revitalised yet again. It's the longest song on the album. Lana's search for eternal love seems fruitless and she admits that the places she's drawn to aren't necessarily the best for romance.

This song is cinematic and has a classic feel. She talks of a lover who is murderous and seems to be paid to kill. She laments the unavailability of the day. It is rumoured that the track was in the running to be the Bond theme song.

The percussion gets big, expanding to include even castanets. The melody begins to echo songs from *Ultraviolence.* The hook is high, mobile and bold.

The slightly lame sounding lyric that is a version of "If you lie down with dogs, you get up with fleas" has been variously attributed to Benjamin Franklin and Seneca. It's a kind of moralist saying, but here it could mean STDs or some other sleaze diseases such as addiction. The song builds to a kind of natural climax. The lyric about his inaccessibility is a moment of intense silence and then a vocally dextrous de-escalating denouement.

Swan Song

The song is immediately atmospheric, drenched in reverb and some kind of synth strings with an 80s feel. The vocal pulls it into Lana's world and there is something of 'Boys Of Summer' here again. She's trying to drag a man away from his lifestyle now that he's made his money. She wants him to come to a world of pure pleasure with her.

The construct of the chorus focuses on them both giving up their work (in her case singing), and marking the occasion with her final song. The chords are strangely breezy before she drops the payoff line. She is willing it to happen. One is reminded of what Amy Winehouse says the night before her death in the film *Amy* (2015) – that is, that she would "give back" her ability to sing if it meant she could walk down the street with no "hassle".

Don't Let Me Be Misunderstood

Lana's second Nina Simone cover after 'The Other Woman' in *Ultraviolence.* The song is an excellent choice for Lana as it lyrically reconciles the two aspects of her personality – the freewheeling and the cerebral. The more anxious Lana is mostly in the past, in the Elizabeth Grant era, but this song is a way for it to manifest without breaking the current illusion.

Additionally, by closing *Honeymoon* with this jazz standard, she makes a canny move that bolsters her authenticity and her claim to the title of "jazz singer". As usual, the inclusion of this track is well-judged and only increases the cohesiveness of the final product.

Miscellany

Dayglo Reflection

A collaboration between Lana and Bobby Womack, iconic soul singer who has been dragged into the future by Richard Russell and Damon Albarn. Albarn's forays into electronic beats and production have got more and more intense since Gorillaz, and Richard Russell has overseen the XL empire which slowly transformed from UK rave into canny modern pop. XL's roster is now huge and has moved far from its rave origins, ranging from the enigmatic Jai Paul to the ultimate post-Winehouse retro crowd-pleaser Adele.

Womack's singing is pinched, pained and impassioned while Lana's is softly sad and reverberated. Her performance ascends to gliding high notes. The strings and piano establish her half of the aesthetic while the stuttering beats are a little too crisp and upfront to be on one of her tracks.

The intro monologue about the nature of a singer's life and gaining experience is certainly on message for Lana. She sings of the surreal nature of reality, and how passing time teaches us that love is the basis of life... and she sings of how she takes her love down with her.

Young and Beautiful

This song was originally registered as 'Will You Still Love Me' but changed to its final title later. It now shares its title with an Elvis song. It was written for *Paradise* but later retrofitted to tie in with the Baz Luhrmann film version of *The Great Gatsby*, which had a great anachronistic soundtrack.

Lana stays mostly within her smoky low register, repeating a sad but urgent refrain.

In the video she appears with two black teardrop tattoos... this could mean she killed someone or was raped in prison. She wears diamond-encrusted hoop earrings – expensive with broke taste. She is intercut with clips from *Fantasia*. She seems agitated but her vocals are soft, 1920s-esque and fit the vibe.

The lyrics reference many of her previous songs, such as 'Bel Air'. The phrase "electric soul" is an echo of "Body Electric". One of the self-infantilising phrases is in 'American' as well, and could be from *Lolita*. The cake she's had now could be the one in 'Lolita'. The phrase about a new world order is taken from 'National Anthem'.

F Scott Fitzgerald could be described as having been preoccupied with the difference between rich people and the rest of us. *The Great Gatsby* also deals with the division between new money and old money (as well as redefining "old money" to even make sense in America, where all money is quite new). Lana is fascinated by these themes.

Once Upon A Dream

This song was originally from Disney's animated *Sleeping Beauty*. Lana's version was commissioned for the film *Maleficent* starring Angelina Jolie, a live action prequel. It sounds like it's coming out of a ghetto blaster that had previously fallen into a river, or an iPhone with a cracked screen. Nonetheless, the high quality real strings that have graced Lana's work from *Born To Die* and beyond are here.

In a curious way the orchestral arrangement and the mad artifice of both Disney and Lana gel strongly. This is perhaps not surprising given Lana's use of *Fantasia* footage in her homemade music videos. Lana's voice imparts a kind of sincerity that goes beyond the kitschness of the original, but the track cages it in. There is a sad, yearning quality to it that isn't explicit in the lyrics.

Big Eyes

Lana's sound and lyrics are applied to an out-of-universe situation – in fact based in reality. It accompanies Tim Burton's film *Big Eyes,* about Margaret Keane, whose distinctive big-eyed portraits were credited to her husband until a famous court case in 1970 – the judge ordered her and her husband to paint. Her husband said he couldn't because of a sore shoulder. She did an archetypal big eyes painting in 53 minutes, winning the trial. Lana's voice in this song is almost operatic.

Prisoner

Written by Lana, Illangelo and The Weeknd – a personal friend of Lana's – and produced by the latter two. A theme of the work Lana gets involved with is that it's heavily atmospheric. The writing and production, while traditionally separate, are here intertwined. The halo – the atmosphere – IS the essence of the product. There is no more focus to be gained by looking harder. That feeling is the work of art.

Two artists whose work discusses the emptiness of love, fame and hedonism finally collide. Addiction isn't glamorised here – it's an unforgiving master/mistress. They swap pre-choruses effortlessly. The Weeknd's eerily high voice is fully weird here in contrast to Lana's low smoky tones.

Some Things Last A Long Time

Recorded in November 2014 for a Daniel Johnston documentary – it's a cover from his album *1990* (which was released in January 1990). She's a fan of his in fact – he's in her hallowed 'Top 8' on the Sparkle Jump Rope Queen MySpace.
She collaborated with Justin Parker to produce it. It was the first time she had worked with him since 2012 – he was involved in 'Video Games' and other songs on *Born To Die*.

The simple acoustic guitar with hand taps and atmospheric vocals are sad and yearning. The track is quite solid at the start but begins to become more fragile and open as it goes on and as a synth cello texture comes in below. The vocal sounds low, dark and mature for the most part but in some lines she modulates her voice like a jazz singer, exactly how Amy Winehouse would twang into a nasal, sassy tone to emphasise disses in tracks on her album *Frank*. This is a very accomplished, affecting cover.

CONCLUSION

We have seen Elizabeth Grant become May Jailer, Lizzy Grant / Lana Del Ray and finally Lana Del Rey. We have seen her confessional folk songs grow tougher, more archetypal and more streamlined, passing through other genres but never settling for too long. Her singing voice falls deeper and becomes more singular. Indeed, when she returns to more stripped down instrumentation in her later incarnations, she seems much more dark and knowing: it's not all about the image and production – a change has occurred deep within her.

We have followed Lana's extensive travels within the US and seen her synthesise a range of influences – filmic, literary and poetic – into a single coherent artistic voice. It is impressive and inspiring from both an artistic and a personal point of view, but also instructive: the thorough trial and error and sheer number of songs written before she even called herself "Lana Del Rey" are awesome in both size and ambition. I hope readers come away with an optimistic sense of what is possible in their own lives.

At the time of writing, the deaths of David Bowie and Glenn Frey are fresh in our collective memory. Both were paid tribute to on the most recent album, *Honeymoon* (Frey in 'God Knows I Tried' and Bowie in 'Terrence Loves You'). Both were massive influences on Lana – The Eagles musically and in their slickly cynical vision of a synthetic, dreamlike California, and Bowie in his constant, conscientious transformation and his desire to experience everything that life had to offer. May they rest in peace.

LONDON, UK
SUMMER 2016